THE WAY
HOME

LESLEY KOPLOW

THE WAY HOME

A CHILD THERAPIST LOOKS AT THE INNER LIVES OF CITY CHILDREN

A DUTTON BOOK

DUTTON

Published by the Penguin Group
Penguin Books USA Inc., 375 Hudson Street, New York, New York 10014, U.S.A.
Penguin Books Ltd, 27 Wrights Lane, London W8 5TZ, England
Penguin Books Australia Ltd, Ringwood, Victoria, Australia
Penguin Books Canada Ltd, 10 Alcorn Avenue, Toronto, Ontario, Canada M4V 3B2
Penguin Books (N.Z.) Ltd, 182–190 Wairau Road, Auckland 10, New Zealand

Penguin Books Ltd, Registered Offices:
Harmondsworth, Middlesex, England

First published by Dutton, an imprint of New American Library,
a division of Penguin Books USA Inc.
Distributed in Canada by McClelland & Stewart Inc.

First Printing, December, 1992
1 3 5 7 9 10 8 6 4 2

 REGISTERED TRADEMARK—MARCA REGISTRADA

Library of Congress Cataloging-In-Publication Data:

Koplow, Lesley.
The way home : a child therapist looks at the inner lives of city children / Lesley Koplow.
p.   cm.
ISBN 0-525-93517-7
1. Homeless children—Mental health—New York (N.Y.)—Case studies.   2. Homeless
children—New York (N.Y.)—Psychology—Case studies.   3. Child psychotherapy—Case
studies.   I. Title.
RJ507.H64K66   1992
618.92′8914—dc20   92-52886
CIP

Printed in the United States of America
Set in New Baskerville and Odeon Condensed

Designed by Steven N. Stathakis

PUBLISHER'S NOTE
The characters herein have been rendered as composites of more than one real person, and the
actions and statements ascribed to such a character are a composite of the actions and
statements of the persons on whom that character is based.

For Those Who Listen

CONTENTS

ACKNOWLEDGMENTS

I gratefully acknowledge the commitment and skill of my editor, Alexia Dorszynski.

INTRODUCTION

When the baby comes," says the Westchester-born OB-GYN nurse, "will you be leaving the city?"

My friend slides off the table, adjusts her paper gown, and assumes as defensive a posture as someone who is pregnant and wearing paper can assume.

"We haven't decided yet," she says curtly, reaching for her clothes. She has been plagued by this question and is tired of explaining why she and her husband might want to raise a child using Central Park as a playground instead of a private backyard. Yet she is compelled to explain. It used to be an easy argument: the cultural resources of the city are unparalleled, the diverse environment enlightened and stimulating. But it's not so easy anymore.

"What about the homeless people? Won't you be afraid?"

I am in the waiting room, listening to this exchange through a partially opened door. I am a child psychotherapist who came to New York City from the suburban Midwest twelve years ago and have spent years making the city home. I do not yet have children of my own, but I hope I will one day. I hope I will know what to say when the nurse asks me the same question. I hope I will know what to say when my baby points to someone in need and looks into her mommy's eyes expecting magic, but finds none that can transform the scene we are passing. I know that there is no stroller awning large enough to shield a child from the fears that this vision of unmet need can engender. I know because I too have felt afraid.

Competing with the muffled voices from the examining room is a chorus of inner voices clamoring for my attention. These are the voices of the children in this story, the voices of many of my patients, who live in a terrifying world—a world without adult protection. They are the voices of some of New York City's neglected children who have come under my therapeutic umbrella for a while.

"I don't understand," a socially conscious friend of mine once said in exasperation. "How can psychotherapy help these kids? They need housing. They need day care. They need nutritious food. They need . . ."

Everything. They need everything. But what I have to give them is less than everything. What I have to give them is a twice-weekly therapeutic relationship, a space that provides a playground for a child's inner life while offering temporary shelter from the intrusive events of the urban world. And I can give them juice and graham crackers to symbolize nurturing and to help them feel full.

With these resources, the children must build their own homes. In the absence of real, functional homes, they must build psychological homes that are strong enough to withstand the huffing and puffing of the many big, bad wolves that have taken up residence in their inner lives. It is not easy, but after some time in treatment most of the children begin to build a foundation. Like all other patients, they transfer their fears and fantasies to the person of the therapist and people her empty dollhouse rooms with scenes from their dreams and nightmares. Like all other children, they present the therapist with layers of symptoms, the most troublesome often fading away to expose myriad hidden conflicts, each seeking its origin, like a set of wooden Russian dolls that keep breaking open to reveal yet another generation. Those generations then become my patients as well.

When the sessions are over, my patients and their families

often return to haunted houses, some in luxury co-op buildings, others in housing projects or shelters. I return to a large, old apartment in a rent-stabilized building with a doorman to protect me. The view from my apartment is unremarkable. I look out from my safe vantage on some brownstones across the street, and from another window I can see the intersection of the street and the avenue, a four-way stoplight forbidding traffic from one street to trespass against the other. But my view as a city-dweller and therapist is sometimes startling. I have an underground view of New York City, a window into the unconscious domain of New York City's children, a view across the lines that divide affluence and poverty, and sometimes graphic images of the ways in which these lines intersect.

In my professional life, I have had the privilege of learning different languages and dialects from my patients and have had the responsibility of distinguishing their inner voices from my own. Deep deprivation in a patient often confronts the therapist with empty spaces in her own person, spaces that have been closed off until a child's cries echo there. These echoes motivate my writing. In writing I find a way to represent both the children and myself. Clearly, children in need lack representation. They cannot vote, nor can they articulate the experience of growing up without hope. I vote religiously, but no one whom I have voted for has been in Washington for a very long time. So I am left to my own devices: dreams and memories from childhood, an urban psychotherapy practice, and a grandmother-taught ability to convert experience to story.

Meanwhile, I continue to live and work in New York City, home to Opal and Qimmy, Ronnie, and the group of little girls whom we meet in *The Way Home*. Opal is a homeless woman struggling to be a mother to three-year-old Qimmy. Ronnie is a high-achieving, middle-class teenager who suddenly becomes school phobic. Maimai, Raquel, Angie, 'Mitri, and Kendra are a group of five- and six-year-old girls who don't remember their ABC's but do remember the violent scenarios that have haunted their early years.

These children live worlds apart within the same city. Yet, in my work I have found that there is much common ground; one well of human strength and fragility from which all the children drink.

I will share this metaphor with my friend when she comes out of the nurse's office, and hope that she finds it reassuring.

But I still can't be sure how I will answer the nurse's question when my time comes.

FRAGILE
FOUNDATIONS

Watch the doors! Watch the doors!" The faceless conductor's voice oriented me to my surroundings. New car. Icy cold air. Clammy-skinned bodies sitting or clutching the metal handholds overhead, smelling at once of sweat and evaporating perfume. A toddler smiled at me from her stroller across the aisle, playing peekaboo between the legs of a tall adolescent. He was balancing a basketball on his hip, annoying a briefcase-carrying woman with running shoes who was wedged against him on the other side. An odor of somebody unclean permeated the car, so in spite of the air-conditioning it was somewhat of a relief when the doors parted at 96th and Lexington, letting the steamy July air rush into the car as the mob of refrigerated East Harlem residents pushed its way out.

I was at home in this mob. It was composed mostly of Carver House tenants, with a sprinkling of white-uniformed hospital employees on their way to Metropolitan or Mt. Sinai. Carver House was the housing project in the catchment area of the East Harlem Head Start Program where I worked as a child psychotherapist long enough to see familiar faces in most neighborhood crowds. Now my work took me to a mental health clinic in the Bronx, a day-care center on the Upper West Side, and an office

in my own apartment. So I had become a commuter, connecting
the various parts of my professional life with rushing subway
trains.

We ascended to the token-booth level en masse and began to
disperse, but I had already detached myself from all feelings of
connection in order to cope with what had become the most
frightening part of my neighborhood: homeless men and women
curled up on subway benches, hands sheltered between their
knees; homeless women panhandling; a homeless woman standing with a baby on one arm and a cup in the other hand. These
people were now living in a neighborhood with a diminishing
rental market and apartments owned by people with means. This
created a polarity more drastic than the confrontation of hot,
heavy underground air with the subway-car chill, pulling the
neighborhood in two. The children fell into the resulting craters.
Scanning the small group of homeless women out of the corner
of my eye, I determined that there were none with children. The
referral slips in my pocket were only for women with children. I
braced myself and rushed past their desperate eyes up to a street
bustling with people who had places to go.

I breathed a sigh of relief as the lock clicked shut. I was
home. They were homeless; I was homeful. I lived in a prewar
building, in a large apartment with clanking steam radiators and
cracked plaster under multiple coats of landlord-bought off-
white paint. There were parquet floors and kitchen cupboards
that only a basketball player could reach. A chorus of meows was
muting the whirring mechanism of my answering machine, which
was taking a message as I walked through the door. I stepped over
the cats to intercept it.

"Hello." It was hard to catch my breath in the sunbaked
apartment. There was confused silence.

"Oh. Are you there?" I recognized the voice. It was Betsy,
director of a private day-care center where I did occasional con-
sulting. She sounded harassed.

I laughed. "Are you disappointed to find me home?"

"No. I just thought . . . Never mind. I'm just glad you're still
in town."

"That's a bad sign." I collapsed in a rocker close to the

phone. "I'm already booked for the next two Wednesdays. After that it will be August and I *will* be out of town." I did one day a week of consultation for day-care centers apart from my therapeutic work in the clinic and in private practice.

"Well, actually I was hoping for something a little more immediate," Betsy said, "like right now."

"Now?" I squealed, leaning over to stroke a crying cat. "What's wrong? Is that kid acting like he's a vacuum cleaner again?"

"No, it's not that. Just come over here. Please!"

I had been working for Betsy as an "as needed" mental health consultant for the past five years, but I had never before heard her plead. I put the machine back on "answer," changed into day-care clothes, and took the bus across town to the West Side.

The Child Care Center was in a church basement. I immediately felt energized by the sounds and sights that greeted me when I pulled the heavy church door shut behind me: cubbyholes full of rest blankets, favorite stuffed animals, bathing suits and towels, forbidden toys like water guns and fake fingernails; giggles and crying hiccups rising from the staircase that led to the basement. Since "graduation" from Head Start two years earlier to work at the mental health clinic, I had missed the early-childhood atmosphere immensely. I breathed it in as I walked slowly down the steps to the center.

I spotted what I guessed was Betsy's problem as soon as I entered the children's space. On a tiny chair between a bustling housekeeping area and the cage housing Georgie the guinea pig sat a woman who contrasted sharply with the liveliness surrounding her. She sat perfectly still with her knees bent, her elbows resting on her legs, her head in her hands. Her upper arms were muscular, and the enormous hands covered her face. Sitting there absolutely motionless, she looked as though she had been chiseled from black stone. A dark gray ski cap covered her hair, and she wore a faded purple T-shirt and gray pants, frayed and dusty at the bottom. The clothes gave off a musty smell as I passed her to get to Betsy's office. The woman did not appear to notice me.

"What's up?"

I startled Betsy by appearing on her side of the cotton curtain dividing her makeshift office space from the rest of the center. The center's space was really just one giant room divided into various cozy areas for the different age groups being cared for— kids between the ages of six months and five years. Betsy had been puffing on one of the plastic cigarettes that are supposed to help people stop smoking. When she saw me, she quickly pocketed it, embarrassed.

"Quit two weeks ago," she explained, motioning me to a chair. Her office was an interesting testimony to the conflicts of a perfectionist. It was lined with shelves containing several clear plastic bins that served as miniature filing cabinets for thousands of index cards. Neatly filed and expertly arranged were cards of every size and color coding essential information on the families served at the center. Anything that could not be converted to symbolic form and written on a card was considered too wild to be wrestled with. The countertops and desks and plastic chairs were grown over with extraneous papers, lost toys, and not-yet-claimed children's clothing.

Betsy came right to the point. "You serve homeless kids in Head Start, right? And that clinic you work for does groups for homeless mothers and kids—didn't you tell me that once?" She looked a little frantic.

I opened my mouth to affirm both statements, but she interrupted.

"Great!" She seemed to relax a bit after hearing my un-spoken answer. She handed me a pink index card with only the initial portion completed. Mother's name: Opal States. Child's name: Qimmy States. Child's age: 3. The address portion was blank.

"They are homeless," Betsy explained, "or at least the mother's homeless. The child stays with someone else. I don't know the details, but I know she's not eligible for any of our day-care categories. I thought you could refer her to one of your centers that has special services."

Betsy's private center accepted tuition-paying families as well as purchase-of-service families. Purchase-of-service kids came from low-income families with working parents who were eligible for some assistance. Opal States, however, was not employed.

"Well, do you have room for her? Maybe she could come in under Preventive Services," I suggested.

"Preventive kids have to be referred through the child welfare agency," Betsy reminded me. That meant that there already had to be an open case on the family reporting abuse and neglect. If day care could help prevent foster placement, children of non-working families could be made eligible. "Anyway, don't get me involved with this, okay, Koplow? You know I don't have any casework services. As it is, I'm spending half my time in the toddler room. I'm short-staffed this summer. There *are* centers for homeless kids. Just find her one."

I looked at Betsy and saw that her designer glasses were smudged by tiny fingerprints and there was a stain of questionable origin on her blouse. I stood up, holding the index card.

"Okay I'll talk to her." I looked at the card one more time. "Are you sure Qimmy is spelled with a Q?"

"That's what Opal said. She didn't say much, but she said that. By the way"—she suddenly lowered her voice a few decibels—"check out whatever is sticking out of her left pants pocket. I tried to convince myself that it was a nail file or maybe a letter opener." She looked at me with imploring eyes and then, taking a call from a buzzing intercom, banished me from her office with a wave of her hand.

"I doubt she gets much mail," I muttered on my way out.

I regarded Opal States from afar. She hadn't moved a muscle. I braced myself for the approach. I always felt shy about moving in on people this way, but apparently Betsy had no time for introductions.

"Hi," I said, sitting down on the edge of the crate that held the guinea pig's cage, "my name is Lesley Koplow. I'm a consultant here."

Opal's hands instantly dropped from her face to her knees, but the rest of her body seemed frozen. The hands had uncovered a constellation of beautiful features dulled by neglect, but the face wore an expression sculpted in steel, incapable of conveying even a whisper of emotion. Opal's eyes looked straight ahead even though I was seated beside her. She focused on the floor.

"I want day care," she said in a deep, hollow tone that chilled me.

"Well," I replied in a high voice, "that's a problem. It's not a problem everywhere, but it is a problem in this center. Mothers have to be working to put their kids into day care here." Opal said nothing. "I know of a Head Start program . . ." I began.

She shook her head. "Only half a day."

Hmmm. She had researched this.

"Yes, you're right. Maybe we need to call one of the day-care programs especially for homeless kids. That way your not working won't be a problem."

Opal said nothing for what seemed like several minutes. Then, "Qimmy not homeless." She said this so low that I almost didn't hear her.

"Where does Qimmy live?" I asked.

"Douglas."

Douglas was a housing project in the neighborhood.

I tried again. "Well, who does Qimmy stay with?"

"Old woman."

I kept inquiring with my gaze, and the inquiry finally reached the corner of Opal's eyes.

"Not really kin, but . . ."

"Someone *like* family to you?"

She was silent, which I took to mean affirmation.

"But you don't stay with Qimmy and the old woman," I continued.

Opal shook her head almost imperceptibly. Her hands were fastening themselves to her knees in a way that revealed that the interview was becoming too much for her. It had already become too much for me.

"Qimmy's not homeless, but since you are, Qimmy might still be eligible for a place in a center with special services."

"Qimmy just need day care, that's all." The low tone had more depth this time, and there was a hint of the desperation that might have prompted this explosion of words.

"You really want Qimmy in day care here and not just any-where. Can you tell me how come?"

"Close by," answered Opal.

"Close by to where you stay?" I questioned. "Do you stay in a shelter?"

She shook her head again almost imperceptibly.

I sat mulling this over for a minute. "There's only one way Qimmy might be eligible for care here, and that is if Qimmy has a C.W.A. worker and the worker refers her for day care. *Then* maybe we can work it out. If the center has a space, and *if* you bring Qimmy for registration and we meet her and play with her and see that the center would be a good place for her, then, maybe."

Opal sat in silence for a few moments. She looked as though she might be permanently affixed to the chair, although I thought the interview was coming to some kind of conclusion.

"Franklyn," she said finally.

I looked puzzled.

"Franklyn, C.W.A. worker."

That was interesting. A C.W.A. worker meant that Qimmy's case had come to the attention of authorities because of possible abuse or neglect.

I nodded. "How do you want us to get in touch with him?"

"He'll call you."

"Okay," I agreed. "Let me give you a couple of numbers." I scribbled my various work numbers down for her. "I have an idea. If he says all right, why don't you bring Qimmy in for an interview next Wednesday at five o'clock. The center's open until six o'clock. I'll talk to Betsy about it."

Opal nodded. Then she stood, revealing her impressive height. She took a few large strides to the staircase, then was gone.

I sat where she had been sitting and rested my head on my arms next to the guinea pig's cage. I felt exhausted. I opened the cage and took the guinea pig out and held him. There were no children around to hold. They had all gone out to the play yard. I felt as if I needed to be holding something, not only for comfort, but for protection. In a minute, Betsy would peek out from be-hind her curtain and realize that Opal had gone, and would find out that I had done exactly what she had wanted to avoid. I couldn't help it. Opal's tone of quiet desperation was more powerful than Betsy's plea. I winced as I saw Betsy heading toward me. She saw the wince.

"Koplow, I *know* you didn't admit that kid." She threw her hands up dramatically.

"She does have a C.W.A. worker, but relax, she may never get it together to call him. And he may never approve it. Relax, Betsy."

"Jesus Christ. If it was up to you, I would have every basket case in the city of New York in here. I don't know why I brought you into this." As she stormed, she was gathering lunch boxes and arranging them to be taken home.

I put Georgie back into his cage. He had served his purpose.

"Why did you call me, then? If you recall, I was at home, oblivious to the situation, and you made me come over here knowing full well that I would end up—"

She silenced me with a gesture. "All right, all right. I was scared of her. Homeless people scare me, if you really want to know the truth. But don't get analytic with me. I pay good money for that kind of torture." She smiled and threw a purple folder at me. I caught it. I could offer no defense. "That's the intake packet," she said. "If we get this kid, you're going to get the information from the mother."

I flipped through the packet. It was ten pages long—more than forty questions for a woman who gave single-word replies, who found five minutes of social contact painful.

"I guess we'll see a lot of you in September," Betsy said cheerfully. "You did tell her it would be September, didn't you?"

I nodded, lying. I'd tell her the next time, I thought. If there is a next time.

■   ■   ■

Opal had gone, but the experience of Opal was still with me, and now it was I who felt immobilized. It was about 8:30 P.M. and I was glued to the sofa when the phone rang; nevertheless, I felt compelled to get up and answer it.

"Hello."

"Hello, this is Jacob." Jacob was a child psychiatrist who

consulted at many of the centers where I also worked. "How's the traveling child therapist?" he asked teasingly. Jacob remembered when I was at Head Start full-time and he always knew where to find me.

"I have a referral for you," he said.

I got some paper ready. "Good. I need a few more of those. My rent's going up in a couple of months."

"It's a thirteen-year-old. . . ."

"Whoa! Thirteen! I was in the market for someone eight to ten years younger than that."

Jacob was unfazed. "It's a thirteen-year-old girl who has become phobic about going to school. In fact, she has been on home instruction for the last half of the school year."

"And *now* they decide to get therapy? What took so long?"

"I'm not sure I can be completely objective. The girl's mother is a friend of mine. We work together on the Committee for Justice in Nicaragua. Suffice it to say that the symptoms manifested themselves physically, so they went the medical route first. Like most activists, the mother doesn't think much of the analytic process. I've been working on her, though."

"Great."

"That's why I thought of you for the girl. You do well with people who have fears about treatment."

I laughed. "Do you think that's because of my own fears or because I've had so much experience luring unsuspecting parents into the treatment relationship?"

"Probably both. Anyway, I do think you should consider this case."

"I don't know, Jacob."

"It might be your first truly analytic case."

"What do you mean by that?" I challenged him.

"I mean, the girl is well provided for, highly intelligent, and very verbal. You don't have to spend hours doing social work related to her basic needs. There's no C.W.A. worker, no survival crisis, no need for weekend heroics to ensure her well-being. You can just do therapy."

"Well, there is the school."

"I told you, she's on home instruction and is scheduled to

resume in the fall. That will alleviate pressure from the school. You won't have to spend much time working things out with them until you get her well. Give her as much time as you can and don't let the case take you out of the office for a good long time."

I smiled fondly at Jacob through the tiny holes in the telephone receiver. "That's an interesting prescription considering that I see private patients at home. To cure a kid who's unable to leave her house, I am forbidden to leave mine."

Jacob smiled back at me through the holes in his receiver. "You'll take the case?"

"You know, I'm going away in two weeks."

"If she has waited this long, she can wait another month," he answered.

I sighed. "Tell her to call me so that I can do a consultation before I go. What's her name, by the way?"

"Weinstein. The girl's name is Ronnie."

■ ■ ■

It was a long subway ride from my house to the Bronx Neighborhood Mental Health Clinic. If I timed it just right, I pushed my way through the turnstiles as the buzzer warned of my train's arrival, thus avoiding the most oppressive part of the underground trip: the space under the ground but above the tunnels, which had become a sandwich of heat and human misery with no escape vent for either. Uptown trains were seldom crowded in the mornings; mine was considered a "reverse commute." There were always seats available, which meant I could make the trip in various states of wakefulness. I sat with my eyelids drooping, my own personal window shades against the sun's brightness during the above-ground portions of the journey. My eyelids stayed open just enough to watch for danger. My mind had to keep itself occupied, since I could never read while riding. Some mornings, words to old songs played in my head, my own invisible radio station forecasting the themes of the day through song lyrics. Some mornings, self-analysis or fantasized extensions of my own therapy sessions accompanied me. This morning I sat inundated by the responsibilities that awaited me at the clinic. Facts and feelings about each prospective member of my therapeutic group competed for my attention. I had been poring over an envelope of referrals from neighborhood kindergartens the day before.

There was five-year-old Angie, whose mother had committed suicide by taking cough medicine laced with PCP when Angie was two. Her teacher reported symptoms of fire-setting, uncontrollable rages, and stealing. Angie had never known her father.

There was four-and-a-half-year-old Raquel and five-year-old Demitria, whose fathers were in prison for dealing crack. Both girls had spent time in foster care while their mothers were investigated for drug use. They were too fearful and preoccupied to learn in school.

There was five-and-a-half-year-old Maimai, whose teenage uncle had murdered her seventeen-month-old sister during a drug-induced psychotic episode when Maimai was five months old. Maimai's presenting problems were enuresis and encopresis; she did not control her bladder or bowels.

There was four-year-old Kendra, who cried inconsolably during class. Kendra had been put in the custody of her great-aunt after her mother's former boyfriend molested both mother and daughter a month after Kendra's third birthday.

I opened my eyes more fully for respite from these thoughts. A three-year-old girl in a party dress, her hair streaked blond by the sun, sat holding her mother's arm, scrutinizing a dark-skinned man with tattered clothing, open shoes without laces, no socks, swollen legs, who was doubled over with his head in his lap. He was several feet away from the girl, at the end of the car. She strained to make sense of this vision, all the while holding fast to her mother, who was busy reading.

As I struggled with the keys to let myself into the clinic, Sonya, the receptionist, was tapping the glass and pointing to the telephone.

"Hi, Koppie. Call on 02," she sang out. Being a receptionist was a perfect job for Sonya. She was so good at making people feel welcome.

"Hello," I answered breathlessly, nearly toppling the phone off my desk.

"Franklyn, C.W.A.," a voice informed me. "I'm calling about the States case."

"Oh, yes . . ."

"We can approve Qimmy States for Preventive Services," he interrupted. "Just let me write down the name of the center."

Mr. Franklyn was obviously a man in a hurry.

"It's a private center. It's called the Child Care Center, but it has purchase-of-service spots. Listen, I'd really like to talk to you about the case before we—"

"Did you get a release of information?" This was a form signed by Opal giving us permission to talk about her case.

This sounded like a tape-recorded response.

"No." It had seemed premature. "I'll try to get one on Wednesday."

"Fine. Call me then."

"Mr. Franklyn," I said before he could hang up. "Before we can do anything, we need to meet Qimmy to see if the Child Care Center is an appropriate place for her. There are no on-site services. I'm only a consultant. The most I can be around is an hour or so a week. Do you have any idea why it is so important to Opal to have Qimmy at that particular site?"

"It's close to her subway station," he replied flatly.

"Oh. You mean she is planning to bring Qimmy by train?"

"It's close to the station where she lives," he explained in a strained tone.

I was silent. I wanted to ask a thousand questions, none of which he could answer without a release.

"Okay," I agreed weakly. "I'll talk to you again after Wednesday."

■   ■   ■

Ronnie Weinstein was allergic to cats. She and her mother announced this simultaneously upon entering my apartment and observing my two large cats, who were both inclined to answer the door.

"What happens to you if you are around cats?" I asked Ronnie.

"She gets hives," replied Sara.

"I'll feed the cats so they don't come in with us," I said. I indicated the way to the therapy room. "I'll join you in a moment."

When I returned I found Sara seated in a soft blue butterfly chair, seemingly quite relaxed. Ronnie sat at the table playing with a magnetic sculpture toy that could be molded into an infinite number of designs. She looked up nervously as I entered, then went back to the toy. The momentary eye contact revealed deep blue eyes. She had reddish, long, wavy hair—layered and pulled back on one side with one of those brightly colored spring barrettes that resemble notebook clips. Faint freckles decorated her pleasant face. Her lips were slightly parted over the braces on her teeth. Her pierced ears held enamel stars. She wore a lemon-yellow one-piece shorts outfit with a Guess label. She worked on her sculpture with intent, creating a delicate dome of magnetic diamonds.

"Jacob told me a little about why you are here." I addressed both of them. "Maybe you can tell me more."

They looked at each other. Neither spoke, as if the rest were self-explanatory. Finally Sara responded. "The doctors feel that the problem is psychological," she began.

Sara's appearance was a lot like my own. She was in her thirties, had dark, wavy hair styled only by a barrette; she wore no makeup. Her clothes showed no labels. Her beige button-front skirt was exactly like one I had in the closet. I wondered how our similarities would strike Ronnie, whose age demanded the forging of an identity counter to her parent's.

"What kind of doctor did you consult?" I inquired.

"A gastroenterologist," she answered. "Ronnie was throwing up every morning after she left for school."

Ronnie seemed to tense at this, but then resumed sculpting, saying nothing.

"It began about nine months ago," Sara continued. Her arms were folded across her chest and she looked skyward as she spoke, as if to remember the details. "She tried to control it by herself for a while by taking Dramamine and Valium." Sara's voice was matter-of-fact.

"Where did you get the Valium?" I asked Ronnie directly.

Ronnie looked at Sara before answering. "At my grandma's house," she said flatly.

"Ronnie spends a lot of time with my mother," Sara explained. "My father died several years ago. He was the victim of a car accident. My mother was out of her mind with grief. She couldn't sleep. The doctor prescribed Valium to relax her." Sara laughed nervously. "It had expired a long time ago."

I nodded. "How did you find out about the medicine?" I questioned Sara.

"About three months after the whole thing started, I saw Ronnie taking pills before I left for work one morning. It scared me." Sara's voice trembled with the first real hint of emotion. "I went to the school to talk to someone there. She had been missing an increasing number of days. She would start out for school when I had already left for work, but then would come home sick. I put her on home instruction and then started looking into it medically." She paused. "You know, I heard somewhere that when people self-medicate it indicates a real need for medication. I talked to Jacob about that. He said that if you thought it was indicated, you would call him." She sounded as if she hoped this would be the case.

I looked at Ronnie but saw no hint of a reaction. They really had the wrong therapist if they wanted medication as an initial form of treatment.

"I'll let you know if I think it's necessary," I answered. "I think we should explore the problem therapeutically before we consider that step. However, speaking of medicine, if Ronnie comes to see me she might have problems with her allergies because of the cat hair."

"I can take Dimetapp," Ronnie volunteered quickly.

This wasn't working out right, I thought. Somehow they had tricked me into recommending antihistamines to a kid who self-medicates.

But at least she wanted to come. "But you won't take the Dimetapp *with* anything else, right?" I said in an exaggerated way. She shook her head, smiling.

Sara looked up questioningly. I answered her unspoken inquiry. "Twice a week; Wednesday and Saturday mornings starting in September," I replied. We had discussed fees on the phone, but something else seemed to trouble her.

"How often would I need to be available?" she asked hesitantly. "My work hours are really long and . . ."

Don't worry, I was thinking, I don't have time to see you as much as I probably should. "Once a month, starting the first Saturday in September," I answered. "If you need something before that, talk to Jacob."

She seemed relieved.

"In the meantime, are you going to do anything fun in August?" I asked Ronnie. "Do you have a vacation?" I said, looking in Sara's direction.

"I'm going to the shore with my cousin," Ronnie answered, suddenly energized. "*She's* a workaholic," she stated accusingly, pointing to her mother. But Sara was so glad to be leaving my office that she put her arm around her daughter's shoulder and laughed good-naturedly as she said good-bye.

SHELTER

Ronnie and Sara didn't have to come with me on my vacation. I'd only met them once before leaving. While Ronnie's self-medicating could have been dangerous, it was not intended to be. It seemed as though Ronnie meant the secrecy to protect Sara from the problem. The self-medicating wasn't a defiant act; in fact, it seemed much like something Sara herself would have done: respond rationally to the evidence of something irrational, like fear. Dramamine for the stomach, Valium for anxiety—all very logical. I didn't have to take Qimmy with me on vacation, either. Opal and Qimmy had not shown for the follow-up appointment after Mr. Franklyn's call, so all I had when I left New York was the shadow of Opal to take alongside the other, more vivid images of my current patients. Of course, I didn't *have* to take any of them along, even those children and parents who had been part of my life twice weekly for some years—or so said an inner voice of reason echoed by an outside analytic voice. But their images and voices usually did make the trip as a way of bridging the initial transition to vacation time for both of us. Afterward they disappeared into the Vermont forest, leaving me free to be rocked by cool breezes in a woven hammock, touched by gentle sunlight, alone or with old friends, unencumbered. When we loaded up the car with homeward-bound luggage, craft-fair purchases, and crying cats, the kids and parents stole back in for the return trip, occupying invisible spaces in the backseat, making their presence more felt as we neared the city.

It was still warm in New York when I returned, in the first week of September, but not hot, not oppressive. I sat on the crosstown bus looking up at the Central Park foliage weaving leafy canopies across the road, still smelling Vermont. Vermont was the perfect antidote to New York. There were sounds of crickets singing at night instead of wailing car alarms. There was time and space everywhere; no appointments; no hurrying; nothing to analyze except the shape of cloud formations against the morning sky. It was hard to come back, but I felt almost ready to check in on Betsy and her day-care babies.

A day of making initial developmental assessments at the day-care center was a sweet way to begin the working year. It was like wading in a stream before being plunged into the tumultuous waters of the multiple problems presented by the clinic population. I entered the church without church-like decorum. I skipped down the steps to the center, where I stopped in my tracks. There, in that same tiny chair, sat Opal States. She looked exactly the same as when I had last seen her except that her index finger was hooked around the bow on the dress worn by a petite child with enormous eyes and a mouthful of fingers—Qimmy, presumably. I felt like a blow-up doll suddenly deflated.

I had to take a deep breath to recover my momentum. Why? Why did this woman who was so paralyzed create instant paralysis in me? Betsy could be afraid; she hadn't had much exposure to people in extreme situations. But why me?

"Hi," I sang out, approaching them. "It's good to see you."

Opal glanced at me suspiciously, then looked back down at the top of Qimmy's head. Was there truth in my welcoming statement? Not yet. In a few weeks, maybe. In a few months, probably. But not yet. Opal said nothing in return.

"Hello, Qimmy," I said, taking Opal's silence as affirmation of Qimmy's identity. "What I'd like to do is have Qimmy spend some time in the three-year-old group so that I can see her with kids her own age. Then you and I can talk for a while, and then maybe we can both talk to Betsy." I swept the room for a glimpse of Betsy's usually ubiquitous form, but I could not find her. Opal gave an almost imperceptible nod.

"Qimmy, Mommy will stay right here. You will be able to see her from where you are playing."

Qimmy gave me her hand and let herself be led away without a change in expression, but I thought I saw her eyes tracking Opal, and Opal's eyes seemed fixed on the bow at the back of Qimmy's dress as Qimmy moved away from her.

The three-year-olds' teacher took Qimmy's hand from mine and gave her a tour of the play space. I sat at the edge of the threes' corner, making mental notes. Qimmy was a tiny, elf-like child, dressed with care in a pink summer dress with matching pink socks and Mary Jane shoes. Her hair was pulled neatly into a bun on the top of her head. When the tour was finished, she stood still in the center of the room, fingers in mouth, large eyes staring at the activity around her, perhaps making her own assessment of us as we attempted to assess her. She made no move for several seconds despite the presence of fourteen curious children. She seemed to feel neither welcomed nor invaded by their occasional approaches, showing interest only in the treasures they held as props for their play. Yet she did not reach for these, but simply followed the desired items with her eyes as they moved about the room in the three-year-olds' hands.

I looked around to find some paper to take notes, and when I looked up again I saw that Qimmy's eyes were focused on a baby doll asleep in her crib in the house corner. Miguelina and Josie were playing dress-up nearby, apparently making final preparations to go out to a party. Qimmy stood still, eyeing the baby doll until the coast was clear. Then she approached it slowly and deliberately, sweeping the room with her eyes; when she felt certain that there were no prohibitions, she snatched the baby from its bed. She held the baby around its belly upright against her chest, its face facing outward, plastic eyelids fluttering. With an expression that I read as relief, she walked quietly back to

Opal, clutching the doll. Opal acknowledged her again by loop-
ing her finger around Qimmy's bow, then raising her eyes to look
at me questioningly.

"Qimmy," I ventured, "would you like to get some juice and
crackers for you and your baby?" Qimmy nodded. I set them both
up at a table out of earshot.

"I think this might be a good place for Qimmy," I heard
myself saying to Opal. But why did I think so? Because Qimmy
had chosen a baby doll to play with instead of something more
mechanical and less human? She hadn't spoken a word to anyone. "I'm going to need a lot of information from you," I continued, "and I will need some from Mr. Franklyn. I will need you
to sign a release of information so that I can talk to him with your
permission." Opal opened her mouth as if to answer but said
nothing. There seemed to be no words today. I presented her with
a permission slip which I had prepared ahead of time. She read
it before she took the pen to sign. She hesitated. "Look at it this
way," I said jokingly, "if I talk to Franklyn I'll only have to ask you
a hundred questions about yourself and Qimmy instead of a
thousand. I have a feeling that answering questions isn't one of
your favorite things to do." Opal's face became contorted with
the effort of hiding a smile. Somehow she had retained some
sense of humor; a very, very good sign.

"Great!" I exclaimed, closing the notebook containing the
permission slip. "Qimmy States is now a member of the three-
year-old group at the Child Care Center. She can begin as soon
as she has her inoculation record in." Opal breathed what was
probably a sigh of relief; but as her breathing rhythms had appeared invisible before now, it seemed to me that she was drawing
breath for the first time, that she had just then come alive.

■   ■   ■

"The case," said Franklyn's voice on the telephone, "will probably come into the system when the old woman dies."

"Who is this old woman?" I quizzed him. "How did Qimmy
come to be living with her? Why is Opal living in the subway and
not in a hotel or a shelter? How did Opal become homeless? Why
is there a case on Qimmy to begin with?" Having tried to reach
Franklyn a hundred times before connecting with him that day,

I was determined to get everything in. I was calling him from the mental health clinic, using the hour belonging to a child who was out with strep throat, which I was hoping not to catch.

"Qimmy States became known to this department on 2/2/87 when an anonymous report came into a child abuse center in Albany reporting a toddler being kept in the subway station during freezing weather. The report was investigated by this office and verified. The toddler was warmly dressed, however," Franklyn added. His voice was monotonous, tight with the effort of maintaining distance from this case. "The mother, Opal States, had recently become homeless. After a brief stay in a women's shelter, the mother and child were then discharged to the Martinique Hotel. That was on 9/12/86. One month later Ms. States came to Department of Social Services and told her caseworker that she could not remain in the hotel. She offered no explanation. She stated that she and her daughter Qimmy were then able to reside with a Mrs. Queeny Martin in the Douglas housing project. This was investigated and verified as suitable." Mr. Franklyn paused to swallow his coffee. The mug banging into the phone receiver jolted me. I had been tense with the effort of following the story. "DSS recorded the matter as settled until we received the call from Albany. It seems that Opal never intended to stay with Mrs. Martin. But Mrs. Martin did keep Qimmy every night. Opal was afraid to leave Qimmy with Mrs. Martin during the day because she's very elderly."

"How elderly?" I managed to ask.

"No one knows exactly, but I'd say at least eighty-two."

"Oy vay," I whispered to myself.

"Anyway, unless this could be resolved Qimmy was facing the possibility of foster placement. But Mrs. Martin managed to come down and convince the worker at the time that she was able to care for Qimmy during the day also. The worker agreed, but advised Opal to put Qimmy in day care as soon as she was day-care eligible at two years and nine months, which is when I believe she came to you."

"What will happen when Mrs. Martin dies?" I asked hurriedly.

"Foster care, I guess."

Now it was my turn to talk, but I found myself speechless. It was a lot to take in.

After a moment I found the words to ask, "How did Opal become homeless to begin with?"

"She was living in a two-room apartment in an old tenement on West 109th Street. There was a fire. Suspicions were that it was landlord arson, but this was never proven. Anyway, the place is a luxury condo now."

This story was making me sick.

"Well, do we know why she wouldn't stay in a hotel?"

"Nothing specific." Franklyn's voice was getting more relaxed. "Conditions there are pretty bad, and maybe she just couldn't take it. She won't talk much, so it's hard to say. I do have a note in the record from a shelter worker who documented that the few nights Opal and Qimmy were there, Opal didn't sleep. She made strange sounds at night, it says here, like a hurt animal. She indicates a concern that there may be history of mental problems."

I waited. "That's it?" I felt tired. "Conditions in hotels were bad so she stayed in the subway?"

"That's it," Franklyn said. "Oh, except for one thing. Every worker notes that there is no evidence of drugs or alcohol. She's clean, and that's pretty unusual for someone in her situation." Yes, that was unusual. Opal had some strengths.

"Okay," I said weakly, having just lost my own strength. "I'll call if I think of anything else or if I have any concerns." I suddenly felt grateful that Franklyn was there. This kind of case was better to share with someone: He could deal with concrete services and I could handle the technical side. We said good-bye, but we both knew we would be talking again soon.

■ ■ ■

I watched Ronnie's approach from my office window. With windows on two sides, the office was the only room in the apartment with a full view of the street. Ronnie walked quickly, seeming oblivious to the stickball soaring over her head as she reached the south side of East 98th Street. She was stopped on the corner by an elderly Hispanic woman who was holding the hand of a little girl drinking from a soda can. The woman showed Ronnie something written on a small slip of paper and they both began pointing eastward in the direction of the hospital. From this aerial view, Ronnie looked poised and mature beyond her age. My eye fell on the little girl as the pair walked toward the crosswalk. A spreading dark stain on the back of the child's blue jeans became a puddle between her shoes, and the old woman began slapping the little girl's wet bottom repeatedly, sending piercing screams through my fifth-floor window. Ronnie caught the scene in her New Yorker's peripheral vision and simultaneously the old woman caught Ronnie watching, causing both to look guilty and embarrassed.

Ronnie sat holding the magnet toy she had played with when we met before vacation.

"It's not anorexia," Ronnie said anxiously as she fingered the toy, "because I only throw up when I try to go to school."

I nodded. She must have been worried about that.

"And it's not what my friend's mother thinks, either." She giggled nervously. "Just because she's a doctor, she thinks she's a shrink or something."

"What does she think?" I asked her.

"She thinks it means that I'm afraid to leave Sara. That's really stupid, because Sara isn't even home by that time. She's already at work. Anyway, I've *only* been going to overnight camp by myself since I was six years old." She pushed her red hair behind her shoulders with a dramatic gesture.

"Really?" I asked with surprise. I remember Ronnie telling me about going to the shore with her cousin. "But you didn't go to camp this year."

She shrugged. "I didn't feel like it this year," she said. "It's a real good camp and everything. I mean, you don't just play like in most camps. A lot of Jewish kids whose parents are political go there."

I nodded. "Well, what do you do instead of playing?"

"Um, you do things like skits about kids in World War Two and sing songs in Spanish about the struggle in El Salvador. Things like that." Ronnie had noticed a bin of cornmeal near the windowsill—a substitute for sand for the younger kids. She was using her silver butterfly ring to make prints in the meal as we spoke. "You know my mom works for Amnesty International?"

I nodded. Jacob was right; I really didn't have to say much to draw Ronnie out.

"She's always too busy with special projects to take a vacation." Ronnie spoke more slowly this time and her voice dropped. "So it's better for me to go to camp or to the shore or something."

"That must be a drag sometimes," I offered.

"No, it's not," she asserted hurriedly. "I mean, it's not like I can't go anywhere without her. It's not like I never get to see her or anything." She pushed the bin away.

"So how come you decided no camp this year?" I pursued.

Ronnie ran her finger over the smooth polish on her thumbnail. She shrugged.

"I must be getting too old for camp," she said finally. I waited. "I wish I could go to school," she said suddenly in a low voice.

"How is school for you?" I asked her.

"Great," she answered without hesitation. She looked both younger and older than her years at that moment, her eyes innocent of the worries written on her wrinkled forehead.

"Do you remember what was going on when it got to be too hard for you to go?"

She nodded. "I was going to be the editor of the school newspaper. That's only for kids who get honors. I'm still getting honors," she added almost sadly, "even though I'm at home. I was going to do an editorial about Nicaragua. I was going to get the information from Sara. . . . They had to appoint another kid by now," she said wistfully. Then, "Is talking to you really going to help me to go back to school?" she asked incredulously. Her blue eyes squinted at me in disbelief. She looked like a very young child trying to believe in Santa Claus after having seen two Santas at the mall simultaneously. Damn! I wished that Sara and I were not so similar in appearance.

"I guess it's hard to believe," I agreed with feeling, as it had also taken me many years to accept that talking could be so powerful. "Maybe for you and Sara both."

Ronnie slipped her polished fingers into the pocket of her cherry-colored sweatpants and pulled out a check; Sara was paying by the session. It was interesting that Sara had chosen to do it that way. Clearly she wanted Ronnie to keep the pragmatic features of our relationship firmly in mind.

"Here," she said shyly, "my mother said to give this to you." And she said good-bye ten minutes early.

■   ■   ■

Tina supervised me as needed on my private cases. A Brazilian immigrant at age five, Tina understood the need to look at behavior within a cultural context. She was trilingual, speaking Spanish as well as Portuguese and English, with a sprinkling of Yiddish picked up from her Jewish husband. She was ideally suited to lend a sensitive ear to the problems of my diverse case load, bringing me the perspective that only someone outside the therapeutic covenant can provide. Tina, her husband, three young children, and two giant dogs lived in Rockland County in a large house next to a bullfrog pond, necessitating my biweekly commute on the Metro North railroad, which rumbled under my urban street and emerged in the other world of the suburbs.

Tina and I shared chocolate mandelbrot at her kitchen table while I talked to her about Ronnie. I looked out the window and saw pine trees whose cones had room to seed and grow. Tina listened to my sketch of Ronnie: thirteen-year-old daughter of a single, politically active mother; full name, Veronica Weinstein; no father mentioned by either as yet; no siblings; has been on home instruction for six months; had developed symptoms of school phobia three months before that; was self-medicating rather than telling her mother that she was sick; honors student in an alternative junior high school.

"Does she identify any precipitating factors?" Tina inquired.

"Says school was great. Her only specific reference was to having been made an editor on the school paper, which made her feel identified with Sara's work. She was proud of that, but somewhere there was a hint of sadness about her need to excel. I don't know."

"What's Sara like?" Tina asked over her cup of coffee.

I shook my head and smiled, puzzling her. I usually loved

this part, painting a picture of the patients vivid enough to make them come to life for a supervisor who had never seen them.

"Like me, unfortunately. Wild-looking hair, Indian jewelry, long skirts, cotton blazers to make the whole image a bit more professional-looking. Like me. Does this mean I have to get a haircut?" Tina smiled, amused. "Ronnie, however, is cool. Guess jeans, styled hair, glue-on fingernails. She's cute. She'll probably be pretty when they take the braces off. She defends Sara like crazy, but at least she can depart from some of that committed image."

"Good," Tina replied. "All we have to do is figure out what it is that she can't depart from."

■　■　■

Betsy was waiting for me at the top of the stairs when I came for what was becoming my weekly, as opposed to my occasional, visit to the day-care center. I was lost in my own thoughts, realizing that I'd forgotten to tell Tina about Opal and Qimmy. The landing was dark that afternoon in contrast to the brightness of the fall day, and I was relying on the slice of sun coming from the slowly closing door to guide my foot to the first stair when I suddenly felt somebody grab my arm from behind.

I drew my breath in sharply. Then, seeing Betsy, I pulled my arm away in annoyance. "You scared the shit out of me. What's the matter?"

"That object in Opal's pocket is definitely a knife. She bent down to tie Qimmy's shoe the other day and I saw more of it." Something made me realize that I was observing one of Betsy's vices, or former vice, I thought.

"What's that?" I asked, pointing to her lighted cigarette. She threw the cigarette to the floor, stamped on it, and finished blowing the smoke out of her mouth from the puff she had just taken.

"Do you hear me, Koplow? I can't have parents coming in here to pick up their kids with knives in their pockets."

"I know," I agreed. "Why are you standing out in the hall-way? Is there someone in your office? Can't we sit down some-where and talk about this?"

"No." I was startled by the abrupt tone of Betsy's usually

teasing voice. "I don't want to talk about it. I just want you to talk to Opal about that knife." I looked at her, perplexed. Her anger suddenly seemed to dissolve, and she began to giggle and sat down on the top step, pulling another cigarette out of her deep skirt pocket. I sat down beside her. "Sorry," she offered. "I came up here to sneak a cigarette, which I obviously need."

"No," I said seriously. "I think it's me who should apologize. I didn't realize it would be so hard to have them here. I mean, you have some purchase-of-service kids in terrible situations, not to mention some of the complex circumstances of your regular tuition-paying kids, so I didn't think a homeless mother and kid would be that different. But I guess it is. I'm sorry." Betsy stamped her second cigarette out, but this time it was to free her hands so that she could wipe the tears that were forming behind her large glasses.

"Does Opal hang around a lot?" I questioned.

"Sometimes," she sniffed. "She just sits there like a stone in that little chair. She haunts me."

"It might help if you talked to her sometimes. I mean, she might become more of a person and less of a ghost." Betsy nodded, regaining her composure. Clearly, it was hard for her to confront someone this needy without a solution to offer. "Is Qimmy a problem?"

Betsy shook her head. "I can't figure her. That's your job. She's elusive or something. She's always on tiptoe, kind of floating around the room." I nodded. "You know what I think it is?" she said suddenly. "I was talking to my shrink about this. You know that psychological test where you have to draw a house, a person, and a tree? The house is supposed to represent your feelings about your mother. Well, somehow meeting someone who's homeless erases everybody's house." She was crying again. "I feel so goddamned helpless when I'm with them. That we let this happen to people. That the government doesn't do something." She had found some tissues and was sharing them with me. Her metaphor was sad. It shattered both parental images at the same time.

"You're right," I said. "No mother and no father, either. The father of our country won't take responsibility for his citizens. He should only know how he is rewriting the story of creation, absenting himself from the image of family." Betsy smiled. Betsy and I had grown up during an era when presidents talked about making war on poverty, when visions of a Great Society were not considered too costly, when the alternative was something we thought we could not afford. The seeds of our professional aspirations were planted during those years when helping professionals were supported by powerful political forces. Now the support had eroded and the powers that be were starving us. We felt abandoned and betrayed, left with a mission to empower people but feeling robbed of power.

"So what do we have here?" I said. "A mother who sits like a stone, a child who floats around like Tinkerbell, and two crying professionals who feel like orphans when we watch them."

"That about wraps it up," said Betsy decisively, jumping to her feet. "I have to go finish the fall roster for the city. Don't forget about the knife," she called as she descended the staircase.

I slowly rose to follow her. I wanted to observe Qimmy at least one more time before beginning the intake questionnaire with Opal next week. I felt certain that at least this initial meeting would take place as planned. Opal picked up Qimmy at five-thirty every day like clockwork. I figured I would intercept her for a meeting between five-thirty and six when the center closed. That way Qimmy could stay downstairs with her group, and Opal wouldn't have to depart from her routine.

Qimmy danced over to me as I approached the threes' corner. She was dressed in a powder-blue version of the sundress I had seen her in last time, but today wore a cardigan as well. "Hi, Qimmy," I said. I was delighted that she seemed to recognize me. She and her baby doll came within an arm's length and then danced away.

"Don't get excited," called Betsy from another corner of the room. She had apparently been watching me watching Qimmy. "Ask Maria to tell you about Qimmy's version of greeting people." Maria was one of the teachers in Qimmy's group. Maria overheard Betsy's directive and laughed as she pulled Jorge's painting shirt over his head.

"She likes the way I explain Qimmy," Maria said to me. "You

know that book we always read to the kids called *Are You My Mother?*" She began mimicking herself, dramatizing the story.

"A little bird fell from the nest. He could not find his mother. He came upon a dog. 'Are you my mother?' he said to the dog. 'No,' said the dog, 'I am not your mother. I am a dog.' The bird went on. He came upon a cat. 'Are you my mother?' he asked the cat. 'No,' said the cat. 'I am a cat. I am not your mother.' "

Ay Dios! I am always reading this to Dewitt. *A el le encanta con eso.* " Dewitt looked up, hearing his name. "Anyway, Qimmy reminds me of that little bird in the book. Sometimes she's going to meet everyone who comes in. The man who brings the milk, the new parent looking around to see if they like the center for their kid, everyone. It's as if she's asking, 'Are you my mother?' Then when she sees the answer is 'no,' she goes back to her baby doll." Maria shrugged. "She is only talking to the baby doll, nobody else, and so soft I cannot hear *que dice.* But Qimmy better start to listen," Maria said, pointing a scolding finger at me. "She dances around here all day long doing what she wants and doesn't listen. One of these days when no one is looking I'm going to spank her on her little *fundillo.* She should listen." I smiled at Maria, silently cautioning her against this remedy with my own finger. "Okay, okay," she responded. "But if she grows up and she don't listen, it's not going to be my fault."

"I'll remember that," I assured her, seating myself in what had become Qimmy's house corner. So Qimmy wasn't settling in as yet. She glanced at me for an instant, apparently determined that I was no threat to her play, and returned her attention to the baby. She was carefully feeding it a bottle of magic milk. As the white liquid disappeared into the nipple and was replace by bubbles, Qimmy's mouth sucked as if she were drinking. Her tongue made soft noises against her teeth. She sucked with an infant's intensity and rhythm. Her eyes were glued to the disappearing milk. "That baby loves to drink," I commented. She did not seem to hear me. Given Maria's observation, I made a mental note to check the medical form that Mrs. Martin had sent to see whether

Qimmy's hearing had been cleared. Finally the baby appeared to be satisfied, and Qimmy removed the bottle. Once upright, the bottle again filled with white milk and Qimmy regarded it with delight. She held it up, beaming, and looked in my direction as if to share the miracle. "That's a magic bottle," I commented. "The baby never has to worry about the milk being all gone. With that bottle there is always more milk inside." Qimmy waited until I had finished talking, then began her feeding ritual once again. Suddenly she was gazing over my shoulder, and when I looked behind me I found Opal standing a few feet away, watching.

"Qimmy takes good care of her baby," I remarked to Opal. Opal gave me a smile constrained by tightened lips. Qimmy stood completely still, clutching her baby and frowning. She apparently did not want to leave her doll. "Play for another minute, Qimmy," I said. "I want to talk to Mommy about something." Opal's smile was gone. She looked as though she might throw up. This was not a good sign given my intention to start the endless intake form at our next meeting. I walked away from Qimmy, indicating that Opal should follow. We stopped at what had now become Opal's territory, the chair next to Georgie's cage.

"Betsy is worried about you having your knife when you come with Qimmy and when you pick her up. She can't allow anybody to bring anything dangerous into the center."

Opal nodded, her face void of readable expression. "Do you have somewhere you can leave it?" I asked. She shrugged. "Maybe you could leave it with Mrs. Martin," I suggested, "and then go back for it." Opal looked agonized. Finally she nodded.

"Good." I felt very relieved, although only time would tell if there was anything to be relieved about. "Don't forget to have Qimmy show you the painting that she made today," I called after Opal. "It's beautiful." Opal proceeded toward the threes' area. I went to Betsy's office to assure her that the matter of the knife had been addressed.

■   ■   ■

Sara's appointment was at 4:45. It was 4:42 and I was stuck in the subway between stations four blocks from my apartment. I sat there, my face impassive, wishing I could kick something. Sara had missed two appointments before rescheduling this one, and I was going to be in no position to make an interpretation about her absences if I showed up late. Damn! Feeling trapped and helpless, I closed my eyes and tried to think about something else. I opened my eyes for relief when the something else turned out to be Opal. Opal was truly stuck in the subway. Somehow the image of Opal seemed to come from my feeling sequestered with my own anxiety and from an anger that could find no acceptable form of release. But Opal was not with me during every subway mishap, so what was she doing there then? I sat brooding in silence, wondering how long ago the steel doors had closed on Opal's emotional life.

Eventually the train got unstuck. "Step lively! Step lively!" the conductor's voice ordered, and I squeezed out the door and through the crowd to the stairway, hurrying up to the street, running to my building. My doorman, Javier, was frowning disapprovingly as I panted into the lobby. I rushed past him.

"*Señorita,*" he called after me. "There is a lady waiting upstairs for you *hace mucho tiempo.*" He looked down at his shoes to allow me a moment of grace, then back up at me. It was Javier's opinion that I should be at home at all times, to welcome whoever might decide to drop by, appointment or not.

"*Si, si,* I know someone's there," I said impatiently, frantically pushing the elevator button. "*El tren me hizo tarde.*" He nodded, indicating that he thought this excuse fairly flimsy, and I stepped into the elevator.

When I stepped out I nearly trampled Sara, who had apparently been leaning against the elevator door. "I'm really sorry," I began, as I fumbled for my keys. "I had trouble with the subway." Sara smiled obliquely. She did not seem impatient, only very tired. I sighed with relief when we finally entered the apartment. But the sigh turned into a gasp as my tabby's sharp teeth sank into my ankle. "Ouch!" I grabbed my ankle. I tried to glare at him and give Sara a reassuring look simultaneously. The resulting expression seemed to provoke a look of righteous innocence in the cat's blinking eyes and a wide smile on Sara's face. She seemed absolutely delighted. "I guess nobody's too thrilled about my late arrival," I commented, holding on to my professional identity like a life preserver. Sara's smile faded and she once again looked very tired. We moved on into the office.

"How do you think Ronnie's doing?" I asked as we settled ourselves in the butterfly chairs. Sara looked at the ceiling.

"I really think this whole thing is some kind of imbalance created by the onset of adolescence. You know, her first menstruation preceded the school problem by only a couple of months." Hmm. That was important to know.

"Do you remember how the onset of puberty had been for you when you were a kid?" I asked. Sara muffled an anxious chuckle by putting her hand to her lips.

"I was nothing like Ronnie when I was a kid," she said loudly. "In fact, I was the kind of kid who seemed afraid of the world. You know, pretty shy, not popular or style-conscious like Ronnie. But then I surprised everyone by going off to join the Peace Corps when I was only nineteen. As it turned out, I wasn't afraid of anything."

"Did you meet Sara's father in the Peace Corps?" I ventured. If Sara was in her early thirties and Ronnie was thirteen, she had to have been conceived during that period. Sara nodded. She did not go on, although my eyes invited her to continue. "I'd like to know something about Ronnie's father," I said gently. "Is he still involved with Ronnie?"

"He sends money," Sara said finally, "but Ronnie doesn't know it." I looked perplexed. "Well, you see," Sara added quickly, "it's not really as strange as it sounds. We were married when Ronnie was born."

"Uh-huh," I responded, not getting it.

"Ronnie was only a baby when he moved out. We broke up and he moved back to the States. Ronnie was devastated at first, but then she seemed to forget. I didn't want to keep rubbing it in by telling her every time a check or a card came."

"But what about at this point?" I questioned incredulously. "I mean, she must see the mail sometimes, doesn't she wonder about the letters?"

"She thinks it's somehow related to my job. He doesn't put his name on the envelope, only the return address." I was left speechless for a moment, which seemed to suit Sara. She crossed her legs and began looking out the window at the changing traffic light.

"How did Ronnie act when her father left?" I had recovered myself to question her again. "Can you tell me about her during the time you described as being devastated?"

"She cried," Sara said simply. "She sucked her thumb, asked for him a lot, lost her appetite . . ." her voice trailed off. While her answer was thoughtful, her affect told me nothing about how she herself had felt at this time. Something prevented me from asking her more about it.

"Did she show separation difficulties when you had to leave her with someone?"

Sara shook her head. "I left her with my mother when I went to work once we got to the States, and she was fine."

"What about when Ronnie was younger? What about when she was an infant? What was she like when she was going from infancy to toddlerhood? When she was beginning to walk? How did she react to separation from you then?"

Sara sighed, this time wearing a dreamy expression. "She was wonderful," she said. "Ronnie was an angel. She had these soft red curls all over her head." Sara hugged herself as she talked. "We knew she was brilliant from the time she started to talk. Her words were clear and beautiful, not gibberish like other babies'. I used to watch her play. She always knew just what she wanted to do and she did it. No one had to help her."

"Do you remember how she reacted to separation?" I asked again.

Sara shook her head. "Nothing really out of the ordinary comes to mind." She shrugged, still blissful in the memory of infant Ronnie.

"What about power struggles? Toilet training, the 'no' stage?"

She laughed a little. "I guess the struggles must not have been too extreme, because I don't even remember them well."

"Well, let me know," I said, as we rose to leave, "if anything else comes to mind about that time." When I looked at Sara to affirm the importance of my request, my eyes met a wintry stare.

∎ ∎ ∎

I was on my way out the door when the phone rang. "Koplow? You've got to come over here!" Betsy sounded wired. "You won't believe what you're about to see."

"I'm on my way over there now, Betsy. I'll be there in about forty-five minutes," I said impatiently. "That is, if you let me off the telephone."

"Forty-five minutes! You'll miss it! Take a taxi!"

"I'm walking. I never get any exercise. I take it from your tone of voice that whatever it is is good, right? So if I miss it, take a picture."

"For God's sake, take a taxi now and go jogging tomorrow."

"I hate jogging. I'll be there soon."

"All right, but hurry!" She hung up and I headed for the park. Central Park was in my backyard but weeks had gone by since I had set foot in it. The asphalt walkways had disappeared under a patchwork quilt of brown and yellow leaves and the squirrels were vying for acorns like frenzied shoppers at a last-day sale. The park was damp because of a chilly rain the night before, and starchily uniformed nannies cautioned their tiny charges about soiling their clothes with wet sand. The promenade benches stretching from the east to the west side were dotted with people who looked as though they had been planted there along with the fruit trees and sycamores that lined the walkway. A gray-haired man with stubbly whiskers and a torn plaid sports jacket sat eating Burry's cookies from a bag. Across from him, a black woman in a white uniform absorbed herself in a tiny book of psalms while her elderly ward sat blanketed in a wheelchair, staring vacantly into the trees. A woman surrounded by bulging plastic bags lay huddled under many layers of clothes, trembling. All seemed oblivious to the promenade traffic rushing past: the denim-clad nine-year-old skateboard rider, the several joggers outfitted in running shorts and Walkmen, the helmeted bicycle rider who skidded on some pebbles and nearly careened into a baby carriage. The passersby in turn seemed oblivious to the bench occupants. I rounded the reservoir to the west side, followed the path to the road, and walked out to 95th Street, five blocks east of Betsy's center. The sky was dimming when I finally arrived, just in time for my appointment with Opal.

Triumphant that I had actually carried out my plan to exercise, I pushed the heavy door open so wide that it banged into a child's plastic lunch box that had been left on the landing, sending it crashing to the floor and announcing my entrance. Everyone looked up. I waved hello and walked to Betsy's office, slightly embarrassed. She was sitting on her swivel chair with a knowing smile on her face. "Did you pass the infant space?" she asked, beaming.

"No. I mean, yes. Well, I did, but I didn't pay attention." She stood up to leave the office, gesturing to me to follow. I noted that the tiny chair next to Georgie's cage was vacant and worried that perhaps Opal would not show up for our meeting. Distracted by this worry, I followed Betsy down three steps to the secluded infant space. The worry disappeared when I arrived. In the cherrywood rocker sat Opal States holding and rocking infant Antoine, who lay contentedly asleep in her arms. Opal was wearing one of the powder-blue smocks the infant room teachers sometimes wore over their clothes, and it hung loose and flowing like a maternity blouse. She sat completely still as always, so that the motion of the rocker appeared to be due to external forces. But her body was not wrapped in the usual armor that was the shield of her strength as well as her fragility. She was the picture of softness. It was impossible to imagine that a weapon could be wielded by the hand that now held this infant.

Opal gazed into Antoine's sleeping face as if there were no more comforting vision in the world. Betsy and I looked on in silence. We were in the presence of a Madonna. Betsy led me from the room. Opal had not looked up when we came in and did not look up when we left. She was entranced by her baby.

"Here's what happened," Betsy babbled. "This morning when Opal brought Qimmy to school there was chaos in the infant room. Ramona called in sick so it was only Cathy in there. Maria went in to help out while I was on the phone trying to reach a substitute. Maria was holding Antoine, who was screaming, when she happened to look up just in time to see that one of the toddlers was about to pull on the telephone cord and knock the receiver down on his head. She handed Antoine to the nearest adult, who happened to be Opal, and sprinted across the room to save the day. When she came back to Antoine, Opal seemed hesitant to give him up, so Maria told her she could stay."

"You mean she's been here all day?"

Betsy nodded triumphantly. "She spent most of the day in that chair holding whoever Monica or Cathy put in her arms. Antoine must be coming down with something. He's never this cranky." I was thinking about Qimmy's play. She was never without one of the baby dolls, always nurturing it in that intense, almost desperate way.

"What does Qimmy think of this arrangement?" I asked finally.

"It's hard to tell. She's been her usual self except a few times when she's come over to Opal's side and stared at the baby like she was an artist planning to paint its picture and needed to commit its features to memory." I nodded. "I even offered to pay Opal today as a substitute, but she told me she couldn't, if we pay by check that is, because she gets SSI."

"She does? For what?" SSI was a disability benefit.

"How do I know? I was thrilled that she even answered me to begin with. Jesus! Don't ask for miracles. I'm telling you the woman talked to me."

I smiled. "You're great," I said.

"I know," she agreed readily, tossing her hair. "Maybe she'll talk to you, too. Who knows." She gestured toward the intake packet under my arm. "Oh. And another thing," she added, glowing. "No knife." With that she waved me on.

Opal and Antoine were rocking and content in each other's presence. I approached, feeling horribly disruptive. "Hi," I said gently, "remember our appointment?" Opal nodded, or else the rocking looked like nodding; I wasn't sure. She didn't look up at me but continued to fix her stare on sleeping Antoine. "Okay," I said, looking at the mammoth form spread out in my lap. "Maybe we should start with questions about Qimmy when she was a baby." Qimmy, who was playing in shaving cream at a table across the room, looked up when she heard her name. I had been speaking very softly. Qimmy's vigilance was striking.

We already had basic statistics gathered from Qimmy's birth certificate and other documents. What I needed was a developmental history and, I hoped, a clue to Qimmy's and Opal's hunger for the symbiotic state of infancy that seemed to define their orbits. I drew in my breath as if freeing myself for the first of many questions regarding Qimmy's infancy, but a deep rumble of words from the rocking chair stopped me before I could begin. Apparently, Opal had been through this before and realized that she had to tell Qimmy's story to the powers that be. "Qimmy born in Saint Luke's Hospital, November 19, 1985. Full-term baby. Seven pounds. No problem. Took the bottle, fed, then slept. Cry when she cut teeth. That's all." Antoine shifted in her arms. I nodded, encouraging her to continue. Maybe it would be better this way; no questions, only answers. Opal continued to talk, her eyes down, her words falling onto Antoine's chest. "Didn't like no one bothering with her. Didn't eat nothing 'cept what I give her. Didn't sleep nowhere 'cept next to me. First words be 'Uh-oh' when she pulled something over on herself. Said more by the time the house burnt. First steps be few months 'fore the house burnt." Opal's tone went hollow and her body rigid. I waited, but nothing else seemed to be forthcoming. I was afraid if I waited any longer she would withdraw and the whole conversation would seem an illusion.

"How old was Qimmy when that happened?" I asked gently.

" 'Bout eighteen months," Opal answered, in a voice that faded into silence. The rocking chair creaked with a lightly accelerated rhythm, signaling the end of this segment of the interview.

■ ■ ■

In a way, the Salvation Army was a strange location for our therapeutic group. The hallways rang with piped-in sermons in the summertime and Christmas music in the wintertime. Captains clothed in navy-blue uniforms nodded curtly to the children as they walked by, patrolling the halls like giant wooden soldiers protecting their domain of fire and blood from the godlessness that seemed to pervade this area of the South Bronx. But the

Army provided a safe, large, centrally located room with carpeting and shelf space, which was more suitable for a group than the small offices of the Bronx Neighborhood Mental Health Clinic. So twice weekly my coworker Franny and I had twenty minutes to transform this empty classroom into a comfortable but indestructible environment. We used the time to push furniture around, set up the play kitchen, dress dolls, and analyze our own lives. We usually accomplished the first three tasks with a few moments to spare, but the last was always interrupted by a burst of sound from the elevator that announced the arrival of our group. Their cries of greeting and protest pierced our sometimes intellectual, always heartfelt introspection, and turned the analytic task inside out.

"It's not fair!" said Angie, zinging her book bag into the middle of the room, narrowly missing the rather fragile painting easel. Four little girls tumbled in after her, sailing past her and pouncing on Franny and me with their own versions of the daily bus mishap. Raquel and Maimai had refused to allow Angie to sit with them. Kendra had tried to entice Angie into her seat by offering her Red Hots candy. But after Kendra opened up the candy box, the bus had stopped suddenly, sending the tiny Red Hots spilling into the seat and bouncing onto the floor in front of Demitria's seat. Demitria had promptly eaten as many as she could retrieve.

"She still mad!" Kendra observed, referring to Angie, and shrugged. Above all a peacemaker, Kendra remained concerned with Angela's anger instead of feeling her own loss. They were her Red Hots, after all.

"Don't matter none, Angie," Maimai said reassuringly, " 'cause 'Mitri gonna die anyhow. That bus be dirty." This apparently pacified Angie, who now felt that justice would be done. She allowed Kendra to take her hand and lead her to the juice table. 'Mitri stood in silence watching these two, then flung herself into Franny's lap and burst into hysterical tears. She did not want to die from Red Hot poisoning. Raquel and Maimai were drowning their guilt in apple juice, which they had skillfully poured from the paper cups provided into baby bottles. They sucked hungrily.

This was our group, considered to be at risk of school failure by their kindergarten teachers, who sought preventive measures for them. The youngest member was four and a half, the oldest member six.

The group met two mornings each week for an hour and a half. The stated purpose was to help prevent school failure by giving children a safe place where they could bring concerns that preoccupied them. The unstated purpose was to help heal wounds that, left unattended, would be "treated" with self-inflicted pain as the children grew to reenact the "forgotten" traumas. These were children whose work it was to remember their pain before they could spell their names, read words, or add and subtract. These were our five little girls.

■ ■ ■

"What do you do if no one shows up?" Ronnie asked abruptly as she settled herself into the pink butterfly chair. She had crossed her legs Indian-style so that her body fit itself to the shape of the chair. Despite the breezy day she was wearing a short-sleeved T-shirt under her overalls, and goose bumps covered her arms. I gave her a questioning look, wondering if she was planning a no-show in the near future.

"Well, you know." She was looking less comfortable and her words were hurried. "I mean, you would be all by yourself in this big apartment all day long." She did not know that I arrived only moments before her session began. "Well, you have the cats anyhow." She looked around. I had successfully sequestered the cats today.

"Are you worried about something?" I asked.

"No," she responded quickly. Her fingers looked around for something to play with, but she had seated herself away from the toy area, so they had to settle for a bead on her necklace. "It's just that Sara hates to be home alone. She'd probably go to work even if she had the plague." Ronnie giggled. She crossed her arms in front of her and each hand grabbed the top of a Reebok sneaker and pulled. She looked as if she were trying to fold herself up like a collapsible umbrella.

"Once in the fourth grade the housing inspector was supposed to come and look at our apartment. Sara had to do something really important at work that day so I stayed home to let him in. The next day when I went back to school I gave the teacher a note saying that I went to the dentist, but the teacher heard me tell my friend Kelly why I really stayed home, and she called Sara at work and told her that she would report her for educational neglect if she ever did that again." Ronnie smiled a teasing smile, as if the idea of Sara being scolded pleased her enormously. This was the first time she had not felt compelled to act as Sara's bodyguard. I backtracked a little.

"How is it for you to be home alone for so many hours each day since you can't go to school?" The smile vanished and one hand flew to her mouth as though to make sure no words escaped without permission. She shrugged. I tried again. "Well, what do you do all by yourself after Mr. Peckwin leaves?" Mr. Peckwin was the teacher the school sent to work with homebound students. Ronnie was silent for a few moments, then brightened.

"I watch the soaps. God, they're really stupid! Sara was right about commercial TV. She never let me watch it when I was a kid, and when I was old enough to decide by myself I was always too busy. I mean, you wouldn't believe how my schedule used to be before I got sick." Her voice had gone up a few octaves and her emphasis was exaggerated. My eyes told her that I would be interested to know. "I was a cheerleader two years ago, um, and last year I was on the school newspaper, and I was in the band both years, and in the junior Youth for Social Change club both years." She was counting on the fingers of one hand. "And, you know, being with my friends." She used up finger number five and seemed satisfied.

"What about after you got sick? Are you still hanging out with your friends after school?"

"Well, some of them. I mean, I always see Kelly because she lives in the Mitchell-Lama too, only a few buildings away." Mitchell-Lama was the state-subsidized co-op where Ronnie and Sara lived, only a few blocks away, "But Paul and Jordana and Ramie live in the Village," she said curtly, as if that explained why they were out of reach. Suddenly she was beginning to look a little pale. The late-afternoon sun was beaming through the venetian blinds behind her seat and silhouetting her against a yellowish glow that made it necessary to squint to read her features.

"You don't like the Village?" I ventured tentatively.

"Yeah. It's nice down there, but they live in the West Village so you gotta take three trains to get there," she said in one breath. The sun had faded, and without it bathing her from behind I could tell that she had become very pale and her palms were sweating.

"You don't like to ride the subway?" She shook her head. She really looked sick. "You okay, Ronnie? You don't look like you're feeling well." She was silent—no words, only a shrug.

"Want some water?" She nodded, head in hand, looking down. I got her a paper cup with water from the bathroom. I was fighting my impulse to tell her to go to the bathroom herself. Ronnie sat with her head down, sipping her water. I could tell she was trying unobtrusively to look at her watch. There were only a few minutes left in the session.

"I think we got to something scarier than either one of us realized it would be," I commented. Ronnie did not reply, only sat holding her forehead in one hand, the cup in the other. We sat in silence. I watched helplessly as she tried to hold herself together when she obviously felt so fragmented. She sat motionless, as though the storm inside had become so violent that she needed to fight the seasickness by holding still.

"Can I leave now?" she finally asked very softly.

"If you want to," I said. She nodded. "I'll see you next time," I said, speaking softly too.

She stood up and walked a straight line to the door, went out, rode the elevator downstairs, walked to the street, and got to the corner before throwing up at the curb as I watched from my window. Then she ran toward home.

■ ■ ■

Ronnie did not come to the next session. Sara called and left a message on my answering machine saying Ronnie had a virus. I was suspicious, given the panic attack she had experienced in the last session and after hearing the story about her having been kept home to let the housing inspector in. But I decided to let it go for a while. Ronnie might need to withdraw before we moved closer to whatever was frightening her so much. I decided to use the extra hour to continue my interview with Opal States.

Betsy was out sick. It seemed that perhaps she too had a virus.

I was informed of this by a frantic parent who was leaving the center with her child as I was coming in. The parent wanted permission to bring the child in earlier than usual the next morning and, having recognized me as a staff member, was determined to get permission from me. It took several minutes for me to convince her that I had no authority to do so, and she finally departed in anger, scolding me for withholding what she was certain I could have given. I was in no mood for abuse. I too was feeling deprived by Betsy's absence. It was nice to have another functional adult on the scene, and now there would be no one but the teachers, who were always thoroughly occupied. I suddenly felt very tired and held on to the banister as I negotiated my way down the cluttered staircase. When I reached the bottom I was surprised to find Opal in her old seat near Georgie's cage. Ever since she had begun to assist in the infant room she could be found either holding a baby in the rocker or walking one back and forth across the floor. "Hi, Opal!" I called out to her. For the first time she seemed actually relieved to see me. She looked up and followed me with her eyes until I found a chair and pulled it up next to hers.

"Where's Betsy?" she asked in a low, urgent voice. She looked as anxious as I'd ever seen her look. Beads of sweat were forming on her forehead and above her lip. It was as though asking the question released them, as words sometimes bring tears once spoken.

"She's out with a virus, I heard. She'll be back in a few days," I said. But Opal did not seem reassured. She continued to sweat in the cool room. I handed her a tissue from my purse, resisting the impulse to wipe her face the way one comforts a crying child. "Didn't anyone tell you where Betsy was?" I asked her. She shook her head. This was interesting. Without details regarding Betsy's whereabouts, Opal seemed to imagine the worst. It then occurred to me that perhaps she had not been allowed to stay without Betsy to take responsibility. "Did you volunteer today?" She shook her head again.

"Betsy needs to be here," she explained as she wiped her face with the tissue.

"I'll let her know you were asking for her," I told her. This promise seemed to help. Opal relaxed to the extent that she was capable of relaxing at the center.

We proceeded with our intake interview, which was based on our unspoken agreement that I would avoid questioning Opal as much as possible as long as she addressed the issues with some prompting. But now there was a problem because we were beyond the point of Qimmy's idealized infancy. I needed information about the period when traumatic events had taken place and ultimately had separated mother and child, and Opal seemed most connected to her memories of Qimmy as a baby. "Okay," I began. "We left off when Qimmy was about eighteen months old, at the time of the fire." Opal remembered.

"Qimmy learnt to walk 'round the time the house burnt." I nodded, having filled that part in last time. "That cause trouble. Had to keep her in the crib in the shelter and she hated that. We left then. I try keeping her with me in the subway station but she try walk off."

"Did you try going back to the hotel then?" I asked.

She shook her head. "Can't live under no one's roof but my own," she said coldly, with deadly certainty.

"And that's when Qimmy went to stay with Mrs. Martin, and you didn't go because of what you just told me?"

She nodded, folding her arms across her chest. I looked down at the rest of the questions: toilet training, separation experiences, etc. "When was Qimmy toilet trained?" I asked.

She shrugged. "Ask Mrs. Martin. All the rest you better asking her."

"Will you sign a release for me to talk to her?" I inquired. She nodded almost eagerly. Allowing me access to the information was apparently not the problem. Telling me, which forced her to have access to her emotions, was another story, a story which Opal States could not yet tell.

■ ■ ■

It was a cold day for late October. Mrs. Martin's apartment was thick with steam heat. The heat waves blurred her short, round body and clouded her thick glasses as she reached over the radiator to open a window. "Gives Qimmy a rash, don't it?" She glanced at Qimmy playing nearby as she served us tea on a glass coffee table. Qimmy did not seem uncomfortable. I felt myself sweating under my clothes as I drank the steaming tea, my skirt sticking to the plastic slipcover on the sofa. I surveyed the apartment while Mrs. Martin went to get some milk. The apartment consisted of four tiny rooms off a small hallway. There was a kitchen, two bedrooms closed off by curtains, and the room where we were sitting. It had been furnished with great care. There was the sofa and a chair, both carefully preserved with plastic, and a breakfront which enclosed some decorative plates and dozens of framed photographs: a few young men with service uniforms on, their close-cropped hair contrasting with the Afro cuts in the high-school photos of boys; a few extended family shots which appeared to have been taken down South somewhere, and many baby pictures. I strained to see whether there were any pictures of Qimmy when she was little.

Mrs. Martin returned. "You won't find Qimmy there," she said, shaking her head. "I didn't even meet Qimmy until she was a toddler. She was named after me, though. That's why her name starts with 'Q' 'stead of 'K'."

That's right, I thought. Queeny. Queeny Martin—with a Q.

"That's something, too, because I didn't even know the child existed till Opal gave my name to child welfare." Mrs. Martin's hand shook slightly as she raised her cup to her lips. I was confused.

"You mean you didn't know the States family before that?"

"Oh, I knew Opal all right. I knew Opal from the time she was a baby. I kept her for a while, too, after her mama died. But I lost track of her by and by, after her daddy's people took her down South when she was 'bout ten years old. I lost track of her."

"When did Opal's mother die?" I asked.

"Mmm." Mrs. Martin's eyes looked skyward behind her glasses. "Must have been Opal was 'bout, mmm, year old, I'd say. Yep, about a year old."

"And how long was she with you?" I inquired.

"Hannah died when Opal wasn't but a baby, just learning to walk. But I didn't get her right away. She went to blood relatives first and I wasn't no blood to Hannah, just happened to be 'round when she was coming up, that's all. They lived right in the C

Building over there, got settled up here." Mrs. Martin nodded toward the view of the surrounding buildings in the picture window. Instead of looking at Building C, I looked at Qimmy, who was sitting on the floor playing with some McDonald's "happy people." Was she listening to this? She seemed completely oblivious to everything outside her play scene.

"Hannah's passing was a tragedy," Mrs. Martin said, her voice cracking with passion. "No one give that baby what Hannah gave her, including myself. Hannah loved that child like crazy, held her all the time. Honest woman. Would have set a good example for her, too. No need, no need at all." Mrs. Martin's teacup was empty and her face was beginning to look drained. I was torn about continuing. There was so much more I needed to know, not to mention the answers to the questions on that damned day-care form.

"How did Hannah die?" I ventured.

"Murder," she answered, looking me straight in the eye for the first time. Her breathing was suddenly shallow, and I was aware of the rise and fall of her chest under her navy-blue sweater. "I heard her screaming from the window and I called the police. Police said it was just domestic. Told him he had too much to drink and walked him 'round the block. She told the officer to arrest him. Said she was scared he would kill her. They told her they couldn't do that 'cause she didn't have no order of protection. Two hours later Hannah was dead. Opal still 'sleep in the crib."

Asleep, I thought, or paralyzed.

" 'Course that wasn't the first time he beat her. Happened almost every time he drank. Turned violent when he had alcohol in him. After that they did catch up with Opal's daddy and he did go to prison. Up there for almost eleven years. When he got out he went down South to be with his people. His mama already had Opal." She began dabbing her napkin on the coffee table, where drops of tea or milk had spilled. Her eyes filled with tears. Suddenly we were both startled by a clashing of plastic. Qimmy had fallen asleep, knocking over the toys she had been playing with. Mrs. Martin began clearing away the cups and saucers.

"That child don't know when she's tired. She falls asleep just like that. One minute dancing all over the house, next minute sleeping so sound nothing can wake her. Happens when we go out, too. I tell her, 'Qimmy, tell Aunt Queeny when you're tired and I'll take you home.' She don't do that, and I have a time trying to carry her, light as she is." Queeny put an afghan over Qimmy where she lay on the floor. I was exhausted, too. Qimmy might have been a Tinkerbell of a child, but her story was anything but light.

"Would it be all right if I come back a few times?" I asked her. "You know, there's so much you know about Opal and Qimmy."

"Any time, honey," Mrs. Martin answered pleasantly. "Any time."

■ ■ ■

Franny and I sat on the floor in a sea of small pumpkins we had bought at the farmers' market. We needed one for each child in the group, plus a demonstration model, plus some extras just in case. We had sneaked the pumpkins inside in a large paper bag. We weren't sure the Salvation Army people approved of Halloween. We sat washing the pumpkins' faces-to-be with wet paper towels, comparing the genesis of our career paths. Friends as well as colleagues, we had a lot in common. We were both thirty-three, both had been professionally driven at a young age, and both had kept a distance from the source of that drivenness until the crisis of the thirties called for a review. We tended to feel both ahead of and behind our peers and felt lucky to have discovered this commonality. "What I think I'd really like to do," Franny mused, "is to open a children's bookstore specializing in therapeutic topics and run bibliotherapy groups there."

"Not a bad idea. It's one of those fantasies that would allow you clear-conscience vacations." That in itself had tremendous appeal.

The door was flung open and there were choruses of "Oooh" when the children noticed the pumpkins, momentarily preempting their usual entry scene.

"Maimai pinched me," Raquel sang out after the novel effect of the pumpkins wore off. Maimai was indeed known for pinching. I gave her a look.

"So?" She shrugged, smiling sweetly at me. "She said 'bitch.' "

"Did not," countered Raquel, smiling in a way that indicated quite the opposite. I looked around for Kendra, who generally took it upon herself to mediate every fight but was strangely absent from this one. She was leaning against the door, thumb in her mouth, eyes on the floor. Franny had already gone to her. 'Mitri came to me to voice her concern.

"Kendra won't talk. No one did nothing to her, right, Angie? She come like that."

"I think she's feeling upset. Did you guys try asking her what was up?"

"Angie tried giving her peanuts but she won't eat none."

"Angie wanted Kendra to act happy. She tried to cheer her up with some peanuts. But I guess Kendra couldn't act happy because she's feeling sad. Sometimes it's okay to let people show their sad feelings. You all feel sad sometimes," I reminded them. Angie shook her head in denial.

"I'm never sad in my house." True enough. Instead, Angie lit fires in the living room to incinerate the sadness she felt. 'Mitri heaved an exaggerated and exasperated sigh.

"I *know* I be sad sometimes, but not like *that.*" Then, having given up on me, she marched off to the snack table to get her juice.

Kendra was indeed extremely withdrawn. Franny had only succeeded in having her sit in a private area of the room. Still no words or tears. "I'm going to cut me a scary pumpkin," Maimai announced gleefully. Horror stories were Maimai's specialty. They seemed preferable to her own inner terrors, so she was often inspired to invent ghostly tales that terrified the other children.

"Then I won't be your friend." Raquel looked suddenly tearful. She was usually the target of Maimai's fantastically gory tales and was easily frightened. Maimai considered this threat for a moment.

"Well, what kind of face you want, then?"

Raquel instantly answered, "Happy." Then she put her hands up as an invitation for Maimai to join her in a hand-clapping game. "Ain't got no food, ain't got no cash," she sang out, "sitting on the stoop and smoking crack. Don't worry. Be happy." She chanted it a second time to Maimai's delight, the last part with the original tune. I glanced at Franny to see if she had caught the lyrics to this one. She had not. She was holding Kendra, who was finally crying silent tears. Maimai apparently followed my gaze.

"Crybaby!" Maimai taunted. She could not tolerate any expression of true feeling. It was as though if any of them let herself feel, she would betray the others, leaving them vulnerable to being flooded by unshed tears.

"Unh-uh," retorted Raquel in a matter-of-fact way. "She ain't no crybaby 'cause she the onliest one who drink her juice with a cup. She act like she grown." Maimai could not deny this, so she for once said nothing, but proceeded to design a grimacing jack-o'-lantern with scars on his face.

"How'd your pumpkin get hurt, Mai?" I inquired. She shrugged.

"Don't ask me. A cut as deep as that, he just glad he didn't die."

■   ■   ■

Ronnie was a no show twice in a row. Sara left messages on my answering machine both times. Ronnie's intestinal problems were worse and she could not leave the house. I made a call to Ronnie. She recognized my voice before I had a chance to identify myself. "Oh, hi," she said brightly, casually.

"How are you feeling?" I asked.

"Not too bad," she answered in a high voice, "but I know I've been missing a lot. I was thinking, what if you came to my house instead, like my tutor does?" She asked this in a breathless way.

"Hmm." I wasn't sure if I wanted to do that. Jacob's words came back to me: "Never leave the office for this one." "I have an idea," I said finally. "How about if I come over and see you for a bit, and if you're feeling well enough I'll walk you back over to my office."

"Okay," Ronnie agreed quickly. I thought I heard relief in her voice. Perhaps she feared I would not pursue her.

The walk over to the Mitchell-Lama building was short. I

found myself becoming increasingly anxious as I approached the building. Counter transference? Maybe. Maybe fears that Sara's decor and mine would turn out to be as similar as our style of dress. As I pressed the elevator button I shook my head, recalling all the home visits I had made to housing projects and tenements with little trepidation. I felt unexplainably apprehensive as I rang the doorbell. My anxiety evaporated when Ronnie answered. "Hi! Come in," she said enthusiastically. "Do you want some tea?" The perfect hostess.

"Not just yet," I answered, looking around. My worries were unfounded. In fact, it was not Sara's taste that was reflected here, but Ronnie's. Clearly this was her apartment. I remembered Ronnie's reference, last time we met, to Sara's discomfort with being home. For whatever reason, it appeared that Sara had really given the apartment over to her daughter. Home was truly Ronnie's domain. I looked at Ronnie. Paradoxically, I thought, she was dressed in jogging outfit and sneakers. "How about taking a walk to my office?" I proposed.

"Will you walk me back?" she asked anxiously, busying her hands with the leaf of a plant that hung from a shelf in the kitchen behind her.

"If you need me to." Ronnie got her coat, left one light burning, and carefully locked the front door. We walked in silence, her hands jammed into the pockets of her down vest, her eyes straight ahead. I had to work to keep up with her. She didn't seem to notice when I slowed down to greet a neighborhood hot-dog vendor. He rubbed his hands together over his cart in an exaggerated gesture and I nodded back—our daily nonverbal commentary on the weather. Meanwhile Ronnie had increased the distance between us by a few yards and was about to walk across the street, overshooting the building. "Ronnie!" I called, then waved her toward me. She ran over and we entered the building together.

"I was thinking"—she spoke while unzipping her vest once inside the office—"that maybe it has something to do with the subway." Hmm. She must have been working on this at home during her hiatus.

"What do you think it might be?" I asked her, settling myself for listening. Ronnie was still breathing deeply from the walk. Was the accelerated pace necessary to propel her from her home to mine? Maybe she was afraid to slow down lest she sense her feelings and become paralyzed by them.

"I don't know. I never really thought about the subway much. You know, you just don't think about things like that." She paused and ran a finger over her polished thumbnail. "I mean, who likes the subway?" Suddenly she was looking directly at me with an intent and hopeful expression. "Could it be *that*, do you think? I mean, if it could be *that*, I could go to school another way. I could ride my bike, or—or something." She seemed genuinely excited by this prospect.

"Maybe."

"Boy, are you smart!" she exclaimed, looking somewhat embarrassed.

"Me?" I said.

"Well, I don't know if I ever would have thought of it by myself."

"It was you who thought of it now," I pointed out. Ronnie ignored this.

"Should I try it? I mean, try going to school another way?"

"Why not?"

"Well, should I call the principal or Mr. Peckwin? Should I get Sara to come with me to talk to the people in the office? I mean, I can't just show up, can I? I wouldn't know what classes to go to or anything." Ronnie looked as if she might jump up that moment, grab her vest, and propel herself to school by supernatural means.

"Maybe you should try making an unannounced visit just to see how the whole thing feels," I suggested.

"Okay," she agreed cheerfully. "If it works I can just come back with the papers and stuff." This was all happening a little too quickly.

"I'm glad you're excited about school, but there are still some mysteries for us to solve," I said. "Like what happened to you when you were here the last time and why it was so hard for you to come back."

"And why I'm afraid of the subway?" she said. I nodded, smiling at her.

"I'll think about that," she promised as she pulled the check from her pocket.

"You can phone if you want to tell me what happened with the school visit," I called after her. She turned around and nodded shyly, then waved good-bye and left.

■ ■ ■

I was telling Tina about Opal's history over decaffeinated cappuccino and chocolate-chip muffins. Tina had come into the city for a medical appointment, allowing for an easy-to-arrange supervision hour. I spoke in a low whisper to maintain confidentiality, getting clues from Tina's facial expression that let me know whether she was hearing accurately.

"Where was she when her mother was murdered?" Tina asked anxiously.

"Asleep, supposedly."

We both have heard that reply many times before. I looked to Tina's eyes for confirmation of what was probably the awful truth. Mine became tearful. We sat in silence for a moment. "How are you dealing with all of this?" Tina asked carefully. I sighed, relieved to be asked. "It's a scary story, but the untold version that I get from looking at Opal's face is more terrifying than Queeny Martin's account." Tina nodded.

"I need to go back to Queeny's," I went on. "I just couldn't get all of it in one sitting. What struck me was the age that Opal lost her mother. It's the same age that Qimmy became separated from Opal, just after learning to walk, during the age of exploration, when there is so much ambivalence about dependency." Tina nodded again.

"Only trouble is by the time we learn all the relevant history, Qimmy will be a senior in high school."

"I know. I don't know how to hurry it up. I'm thinking about spending time with Qimmy at the center on a regular basis. Maybe trying to facilitate some interaction between Opal and Qimmy since they're both there. I'll probably never get them into my office." Tina agreed. Qimmy was not formally "my patient," but the subject of a consultation.

I then proceeded with an update on Ronnie, highlighting the panic attack, her absence from treatment, her insight about the subway.

"I have to tell you a dream I had about you and Ronnie," Tina said. "She comes for a session but she doesn't want to leave when the session is over so you talk to her about it. You look away for one second, and when you look up again Ronnie has become a faded printed design on your butterfly chair."

I chuckled. "And there she stays until the next session."

"Presumably. I woke up before that part." Tina laughed.

"Hmm. So I'm left safeguarding the soul of Ronnie, or maybe she feels like she needs to leave me with the prettiest part of herself."

"She needs to give that part of herself to you because she's afraid of what will happen if she leaves a space for herself, if she's not you and she's not Sara."

I protested. "I don't really think she's that attached to me, not yet anyway."

"Think again," advised Tina, sipping her drink. "Think again."

■ ■ ■

Betsy had concerns about Qimmy that went beyond the "not listening" reported by Maria. She convinced me to change my schedule one week in order to spend an entire morning observing Qimmy. There were jingle bells threaded into the shoelaces of Qimmy's shoes. This was Maria's idea. "For two reasons," Maria explained. "So she doesn't wander off outside and nobody notices. Second, like, hmm, you put a bell on the collar of a pussycat so the little bird can fly away before the cat pounces, *tu sabes?*"

Who was Maria afraid Qimmy would pounce on?

"It's not who, it's what. You name it, Qimmy takes it. Not to play, really; except for the baby doll, she doesn't play, she just wants to hold everything. *Dios mio!* If she's not holding everything in the room, then she's putting everything in her mouth." With her behavior characteristic of a younger child, Qimmy had obviously managed to exasperate Maria.

Qimmy jingle-jangled her way around the room. She reminded me of a whimsical baby spider, weaving intricate lines from one spot to another, dangling near enough to the others to glimpse their play, then grabbing something that she found sustaining for the moment before retreating to her web and becoming invisible once again. Did she even notice the reaction she invited? She had to be taking it in, because her own behavior had changed upon confrontation. Initially, she had stood seemingly bewildered and passively surrendered whatever object Maria had been commissioned to retrieve. Now she voiced protest. "That's mine!" And sometimes, *"Da me lo,"* using the Spanish words she heard her victims say when she took their things.

"No," Maria would explain patiently. "That is not yours. Monica is using that right now. You have to wait." But this did not seem to register with Qimmy. She had the ears of a two-year-old when it came to matters of ownership.

This time Qimmy had her eye on a train for which Marky and Benjamin were creating tracks and tunnels. They had wooden houses and people and animals clustered at the make-believe stations. Qimmy tiptoed over to them. "My train," she said softly. The boys looked at each other nervously.

"Can Qimmy play with you guys?" I asked. I wanted to see what would happen. Reluctantly Benjamin moved closer to Marky, making space for Qimmy at one end of the track.

"Use those," he instructed, pointing to a basket of not-yet-assembled train cars. Qimmy looked them over, then sat down gingerly and began assembling the magnetic cars. Maria glimpsed this activity, then raised her eyebrows at me, indicating that this was something new. She put her finger in front of her lips as if to prevent herself from commenting and perhaps disturbing Qimmy's concentration. But Qimmy seemed oblivious to our attention. She had gone to the block shelves and was collecting large, semicircular blocks. She brought these back to the track and leaned over so that we could not see the scene that was evolving. I looked down to make some notes about the play. When I looked up again she had abandoned the toys.

"Qimmy went to snack," Marky informed me. I scanned the room and found Qimmy seated with three other little girls at a table on the other side of the room for juice and graham crackers. I got up to examine Qimmy's creation. A very long train sat on a track inside an equally long tunnel. Tiny wooden people stood beside the tracks. No animals, no miscellaneous objects. This, it seemed, was Qimmy's still life view of her mother's underground home, the last home that she and Opal had shared.

■   ■   ■

"My girlfriend's mother says I should tell you my dreams," said Ronnie with a nervous giggle. I waited, looking interested enough for her to pursue this if she wanted to. "Well, I'm in this really dark tunnel. It looks a little like the subway at 168th Street." I was beginning to feel a little claustrophobic in reaction to all this subway imagery; between Ronnie, Qimmy, Opal, and my own daily transportation experience it seemed as if I were being sequestered underground. I took a deep breath to fight the claustrophobic feeling.

Ronnie continued. "It's really dark and no one else is there, just me. Then I see these two lights shining at me from the tunnel, and at first I feel relieved; I think it's just the train coming. But then they start getting closer and closer. They look like giant eyes. But when they get really close they could turn into, well, I guess mirrors, black mirrors. I can see myself in both of them and it seems like somehow I'll get stuck behind them and I won't be able to come out. Then I wake up." She was breathless, looking at me expectantly. "Well, aren't you supposed to tell me what it means or something?" She was twisting a lock of red hair in front of her chest.

"Well, it works better if we figure it out together. Did you dream this last night?" She nodded. "Do you remember how you felt in the dream?"

"Scared," she said flatly.

"Of what?" I questioned.

"The eyes. I mean, the lights. Well, the whole thing." Silence for a moment. "Oh, by the way, I went to visit school yesterday," she said brightly, neatly deflecting the conversation about the subway.

"You did? How was it?"

"Good. I felt scared when I left the house but as soon as I got on my bike I felt okay."

"Did you go in?"

She shook her head. "I would have, but I don't know, I felt shy or something. But tomorrow Sara and I have an appointment to go back. She said she'll call you." I nodded. A long pause followed. Then, "I'm not telling anyone I'm afraid of the subway. I'm telling them I got a new kind of medicine that helps my stomach."

"Well, I guess therapy's a new kind of medicine for you." Ronnie smiled broadly, her braces glistening in the afternoon light.

"Right," she said, nodding in agreement. "Right."

"And how do you think it will be to be back in school?" I wondered aloud.

"A relief," answered Ronnie. "I'll have freedom."

■ ■ ■

Mrs. Martin was going to come to the center to continue giving me Qimmy's history. She wanted to check out the place where Qimmy spent her days and decided that this would be a good way to kill two birds with one stone. But at the last minute she called to change the plan. The elevator in the project was not working. She was afraid she would be stuck twelve floors away from home, unable to climb the steps. She requested that I make a home visit. This time Qimmy was at school while I was at Mrs. Martin's apartment.

"I'm glad of that," Mrs. Martin confided. "Never do know how much she's understanding just the same." She was a wise woman; many people assume young children are oblivious to anything not addressed to them directly.

"Qimmy reminds me so much of Opal when she was a child. Sometimes I catch myself getting ready to call out 'Opal' instead of 'Qimmy.' "

"Really? In what ways are they alike?" This was fascinating to me. Mrs. Martin thought a moment.

"In a way that you never know what Qimmy be thinking, whether she's paying you any mind or not. Opal was like that, too. Maybe Opal should have gone to school young like Qimmy's doing now. I don't know. She grew up quiet, though. Never asked much about her mama. Never spoke up much in school. Even still, she did learn to read. I think she may be real smart. The school told me to have her tested. But then that was just before her people come and took her." Mrs. Martin shook her head and stared out the window for a moment. I wasn't sure whether she could see far enough to be looking into the courtyard or whether the window just offered a better retrospective view. "Opal had bad dreams as a child. Used to make funny noises in her sleep, wake up crying, couldn't say what scared her. Now that's one way Qimmy and Opal are opposites. Qimmy would sleep through the Second Coming." She chuckled and we smiled at one another.

"That's what Mr. Franklyn said happened when Opal and Qimmy tried to stay at the shelter. Opal would cry at night and make strange noises. She never closed her eyes, either. The worker said it was almost like she was sleeping with her eyes open." Mrs. Martin folded her arms across her chest and nodded.

"I remember Hannah taking naps with Opal in the afternoon 'cause Opal's daddy would be gone then. At nights when he drank, that's when the violence came out. Hannah said she was afraid to go to sleep with him that way. Sometimes I wonder what Opal's life was like down South. After all, she was with her daddy's people, and then when he got out of prison he went down there. I don't know how much he changed."

"Did Opal tell you about her life down South after you reconnected?"

"Hardly a word, but after C.W.A. agreed for Qimmy to come to stay with me I tried to convince Opal to do the same. She refused. Finally she told me she couldn't stay 'cause Kevin was living here." Kevin was Mrs. Martin's eighteen-year-old grandson. "I told her 'Kevin won't bother you. I'll be right here.' But Opal wouldn't talk no more about it. I guess the way she see it, I couldn't protect her from her daddy, so how am I going to protect her from anyone else?"

What a paradox. Opal was afraid of being attacked at Mrs. Martin's house, so she took refuge in the subway where there can be no pretense of safety. I wonder if this was a parallel to Maimai's fascination with horror films. Each sought an external environment that mirrored her inner state. Faced with the loss of her housing and the unavailability of another apartment, Opal sought a space where she would actually be as unprotected as she felt. I came back to Mrs. Martin.

"You have given Opal everything that you could have given her." I read guilt in her watery eyes.

"At least she can use this address to receive the SSI checks that Mr. Franklyn got for her due to her conditions."

I nodded.

"I'll tell you something else," she said to me in a husky whisper. Perhaps she wanted to be sure that Kevin would not be able to hear her. "I want to give Opal this apartment. I mean, when I'm gone. When I'm gone to the Lord. I want her and Qimmy to stay here. I want to do it legal so they don't get tossed out first time Housing comes around to inspect. I don't know how to go about it, though. I asked Franklyn, but he said he didn't know the regulations 'cause that wasn't his domain." She squinted at me through her glasses. "Can you help me?" It was a great idea. Just the kind of idea that had no possibility of working.

"Well," I said, "I'll help you to find out about it," trying not to sound too hopeful.

"That's a start," Mrs. Martin replied. "That's a start."

■ ■ ■

The first snow of the season came in on the bottom of their shoes and boots, clinging to their mittened hands and thick braids, dropping off and melting into soft puddles on the Salvation Army's carpet. "Look, y'all!" exclaimed Kendra, pointing through the window. "Those are our footprints." They all pressed their noses against the gated window to look down to the street where the bus had left them off, always amazed to see evidence of their own impact on anything.

"My baby's sick," announced Maimai, who had become disenchanted with window-gazing. She pulled her snow clothes off and tossed them on the radiator to dry. "My baby caught a chill from this weather." She picked up a large black doll from the doll bed and held her tenderly. "Somebody be the doctor."

"Me," said 'Mitri. "Just come over here to my waiting room till I call you." Maimai took a seat with her baby and waited patiently.

"Well?" Maimai demanded finally.

"You can bring her in. What's the matter with her anyhow? Didn't you give her enough water?" Doctor 'Mitri demanded.

"Yes, I did. That's how she got sick to begin with. Keeps drinkin' too much water. She want it *all* the time." This was an interesting symptom for Maimai's baby to have, since Maimai's presenting problems were enuresis, encopresis, and lack of ability to retain what she learned in school. It seemed that Maimai's mother's unacknowledged feelings for her murdered baby had been passed on to Maimai, who passed them out of her body.

"All right," 'Mitri interrupted impatiently, tired of dealing with this particular patient's mother. "All right. All right. Here— take two Medicaid cards, then. Don't give her no more water and come back if her fever get high."

"If her fever get too high she could die," Maimai said solemnly.

"What will you do then?" inquired 'Mitri with interest.

Maimai shrugged. "Get a new baby, I guess," she said without feeling.

"You stupid boba! You stupid boba!" raged Angie. "Babies do not die." Suddenly she rushed into the house area with a dripping paintbrush in her hand, ready to attack Maimai. Angie had been peacefully painting a moment before, but she could not tolerate discussion of death. Her own suicidal feelings were still disassociated, expressed only by striking matches held too close to her bedspread. I jumped up and grabbed her hand, which further enraged her. She dropped the brush and began kicking and hitting at me so that I needed to restrain her from behind.

"Angie, Maimai and 'Mitri are playing about their baby being sick and dying and that upsets you."

Angie continued to flail, screaming "No!" and crying hard.

Kendra flew into distress, hovering over Angie anxiously. "Angie, stop it, please. I'll give you my crackers, Angie. I'll be your friend. Don't cry. Maimai didn't mean it, did you, Maimai?"

Maimai was standing absolutely still, her baby dangling from one hand, despair in her eyes. She shook her head in response to Kendra. Franny was behind 'Mitri, praising her for refraining from beating Angie, her usual response to Angie's rages. 'Mitri sucked her fingers and leaned against Franny. Raquel buried her head in a pillow in the soft corner, her hands over her ears, sucking her bottle. Kendra knelt next to Angie, petting Angie's hair, and for a moment the only sound was Angie's quieting sobs.

■   ■   ■

I had fifteen minutes between patients, so I phoned Franklyn to tell him about Mrs. Martin's idea to leave her apartment to Opal. "Oh, man!" said Franklyn. "That's a very nice idea. Now tell her to forget it. Martin isn't even *related* to the States. No way in hell Housing will transfer that apartment. And she can't just ease in, because when Martin dies it will be public record. Opal and Qimmy will be out in a week."

"I know. I know. But didn't you tell me Opal was on the list for that project?"

"Yeah, for that project and a hundred others. Not for that particular apartment."

"Well, all right. But if she's on the list that means she's been approved as eligible, right?" I was eating a Chunky, which was helping me to be persistent.

"Yeah, she's eligible. In fact, she's a priority because she's homeless. But so are another one hundred thousand or so people in New York City. Things just don't work that way."

I mulled this over for a minute. "Well, if Mrs. Martin was a blood relative to Opal, then could she have the apartment?"

"I'm not sure. You could call Housing anonymously. I don't know. If it was a rent-stabilized apartment then she could, but for a housing-project apartment, I don't know. Don't count on it. Anyway, what good would that do? You going to doctor her birth certificate? Supply her with fake identification?"

"No, no, nothing that's not kosher. Well, maybe a little. I'll let you know what they say."

"You do that," Franklyn advised. "I'm going to need to talk to my supervisor about this. Anyway, we would need to determine whether Opal is able to take care of Qimmy at this point. But that's a premature question because I don't think this scheme will work. You better start calling now if you want to find out anytime soon. You might get an answer by Christmas."

"I will," I said. "Right now." And I would have, except that Sonya buzzed me to tell me to pick up the other line.

"Koplow, do you know what happened here today?" It was Betsy. "She whacked a kid. I nearly put Maria on probation last month for slapping Qimmy's hand and Opal goes and whacks a two-year-old kid hard, in front of everyone. What happens if Peter goes home and says something to his mother? I could be in serious trouble here."

"Hmm." I was trying to picture what Peter could have done that would have mobilized Opal's rage. "What was Peter doing?"

"Crying. He was crying and screaming after his mother left, starting to pull things off the shelf and throwing them. Cindy had her hands full at the time and asked Opal to come from the infant room to help. Cindy said she saw Opal come over in her silent heavy way, stare down at Peter tantrumming, and then before she knew it Opal smacked him hard on the behind. Cindy got scared and called me. Opal disappeared by the time I came out of the office. Damn it!" Betsy had been shouting. Now she just sounded weary and defeated. "I just can't take this kind of risk."

"Well, having Qimmy with you is one thing, Opal is another."

"I know. But it seemed like such a good idea. She seemed so good with the babies. She *is* good with the babies."

"But maybe only little babies. Maybe not toddlers. Maybe the staff needs to be educated about the ways that it can use Opal."

"She needs more care than she can give, that's for sure." Betsy sighed. "You're sure she's not on crack or something, aren't you?"

"Both Franklyn and Mrs. Martin say no." I thought of Opal in the shelters sleeping with her eyes open. "Probably she's not. She's too afraid of losing control," I assured Betsy. I couldn't see Opal being able to let go of reality for the escape that drugs would provide. Her experiences had taught her that loss of contact with reality was much too dangerous. "That's why she can't be with two-year-olds," I said, thinking aloud. "She probably had to squash Peter because he brought up her own dependency needs that she's worked so hard to control."

"Well, she's doing a great job with that, if you ask me, because she needs to go and stay with Mrs. Martin and she won't. I can't stand to think of her in the subway freezing all night. Christmas is coming. We're making all these little decorations for the kids to take home. She sits there rocking the babies and watching the big kids making Santa Claus stockings. I just . . . I don't know. What's going to happen to her?" Betsy's voice was strained.

"Are you crying?"

"Just cut it out! I told you, you're not my shrink."

"I wasn't being your shrink. I was being your friend."

"Oh." There was a pause. "In that case, yes."

"Let me tell you something that Mrs. Martin told me. She wants Opal to have her apartment when she dies. She wants Franklyn and me to figure it out. Logistically, I mean."

"Could that work?" Hope was creeping back into Betsy's voice.

"I don't know. I'm checking into it. But what we need to figure out is whether we think Opal and Qimmy would be safe together if they did have an apartment. That is, safe without Queeny Martin."

"What do you mean?"

"I mean it's one thing to get an apartment and another thing to make a home for a three-year-old child when your own concept of home has been shattered. Being with babies and being with toddlers seems to be a whole other realm for Opal. Qimmy is not a baby anymore."

"Well, can you repair that concept of home somehow? I mean, is it too late?" In my mind, I heard Mrs. Martin's voice telling the story of Opal.

"We'll see," I said. "I guess we'll see."

■ ■ ■

Sara Weinstein was in my office at 7:15 A.M. for a before-work appointment. I was dressed as though I were an at-work professional, but in reality I was not quite awake. I was becoming mesmerized by the curl of steam rising from Sara's take-out cup of coffee, which she held in front of her with both hands.

"It's just as though the whole thing never happened," Sara was saying with relief in her voice. "We went in, registered, got her schedule, and she went to class without any difficulty. I'm really

so grateful." She sipped from her cup of coffee. I struggled to
organize a response, having gradually tuned in enough to hear
what Sara was saying.

"I'm delighted that she was able to go back," I responded
enthusiastically. There was a pause.

"I do realize that there are still some problems, and of course
I want her to continue with you until those are cleared up," Sara
added. I nodded. She set her coffee down and gave me a skeptical
look. "I really don't understand this business about the subway."
She folded her arms across her chest. "Ronnie's been riding the
subway since she was tiny. She was never afraid."

"What did make her afraid when she was little?" I asked.

"Not a thing. She was almost fearless. I mean, I remember
taking her to the country when she was three years old and my
mother laughing because she always ran so far ahead of us.
Seemed as though she had already been there and was showing
us the way." Sara looked into the Monet print on the wall above
my head. "I remember thinking to myself, 'It's because she was
conceived during the time I was in the Peace Corps, while I was
feeling brave and powerful and free of the doubts that plagued
me in my high-school years. That's the reason Ronnie's so independent.' " She again looked at me directly, this time with a
pleading expression. "Why is that changing now? Why is she
acting so paralyzed? I mean, she's so competent. She's good at
everything. I felt so incompetent as a kid. It took the Peace Corps
to show me what I was really capable of doing."

"Maybe there's something that's making Ronnie feel incompetent. I don't know what it is, but in the meantime it sounds like
it feels scary to have her suddenly seem so fragile." Sara blinked.
The blink looked like the blink of Jeannie on the TV show *I Dream
of Jeannie,* a blink that transported her to somewhere distant from
my office. After what seemed like a very long time, Sara spoke.

"Adolescence is a difficult time for everyone," she said softly.

■ ■ ■

Opal hadn't shown up at the Child Care Center since the incident
with Peter. Qimmy missed three days in a row, until Betsy called
Mrs. Martin and arranged for another parent who lived in the
same project to bring Qimmy when she brought her own child to

school. Queeny Martin was also worried about Opal. She hadn't been by to visit Qimmy or to eat her evening meal. Besides, Queeny had some news for Opal. Queeny's grandson Kevin had been invited down South to visit his cousins for the Christmas holidays. Queeny wanted to let Opal know about this and to see if she could convince Opal to stay with her for Christmas while Kevin was gone.

After hearing an update from Betsy, I went to spend some time with Qimmy. She was sitting in a tiny rocking chair, rocking one of her baby dolls, when I approached. She got up as soon as she saw me and walked over to me with what looked like intent. "Mommy," she whimpered. She dropped the baby and rubbed her face with her fist like a fussy infant who is tense with discomfort.

"Qimmy wants Mommy," I reflected, "and she hasn't come in so many days." Qimmy looked at me hopefully, apparently waiting for me to produce Opal. "Do you want to go and try to find Mommy?" I said on an impulse. Betsy raised her eyebrows at me from the easel, where she was helping secure a new pad of paper for Margarita. "We'll go to Opal's subway station and check out whether she's there," I said by way of explanation to Qimmy and Betsy. "If she's not there, we'll come back and tell Betsy," I said to Qimmy as I led her to her cubbyhole to start the long process of fitting her into her winter clothes. "If she is there, we'll try to bring Opal back with us." Betsy's wave approved the plan, and Qimmy and I set out on our journey.

The day was cold and damp and the street was crowded with cold, damp, and disgruntled shoppers who had hoped that everyone else would still be at work instead of jamming the sidewalks and stores. Qimmy pointed in the direction of the Christmas-tree vendor across the street. "Look at the Christmas trees!" I exclaimed. She said nothing but kept pointing, perhaps at the bearded man selling the trees, who might have looked something like Santa to her. "We'll see if Mommy is here," I said as I held her hand to help her down the steep steps to the subway.

A stinking man sitting on the cold concrete beside the token booth was the first person we saw. I looked at Qimmy's face. She did not seem to see him but was actively scanning the station, presumably for Opal. This was the most focused I had ever seen Qimmy. I didn't see Opal, but then I wasn't sure exactly where she would be. I fumbled in my bag for a token so that we could pass through the turnstile and look for Opal on the platform. This meant that I momentarily let go of Qimmy's hand, and she instantly slipped under the bar and headed downstairs. "Qimmy!" I yelled, zooming through to grab her. "You have to stay with me! You can't go by yourself." My voice was stern. Her speedy departure had scared me. But Qimmy made no visible response to the tone of reprimand or to the message. I held her wrist in a no-escape grip and we proceeded. "Qimmy, I don't want you to get lost. I want you to stay safe when we're outside." Again no response.

The platform was not particularly crowded at this time of day. Clearly, Opal was not here. I looked across to the uptown track. Someone was seated on a milk crate under one of the staircases facing the local track. I could not see the front of the person, but it looked like a tall woman wearing an oversized coat. "Come on, Qimmy, let's go around to the other side. Let's see if that's Mommy over there." Qimmy picked up on my quickening pace and together we ran down the steps, through the tunnel, and up the steps again. Qimmy smiled as we ran together, as though the synchrony were something she had never experienced before and found both safe and exhilarating.

The buzzer forecasting an approaching train began to sound as we stepped onto the platform, and two trains simultaneously barreled up the express and local tracks, doors opening to let passengers transfer. In the confusion I caught sight of Opal out of the corner of my eye. It had been she on the crate. She was about to board the number 1 uptown local.

"Opal!" I called out, but she did not hear.

"Come on, Qimmy." I boosted her into the closest car as the doors closed. "We're going to walk through the train and find Mommy."

Qimmy was an expert at walking through the moving cars. Although I kept holding her wrist, she didn't lean on me for balance and never lost her footing. I was nervous. I rarely walked through the moving train myself and had never done so with a child, but I didn't want Opal to get off before we found her. I saw Opal through the glass as I opened the doors into the middle car, the trainman's car. She was sitting in the far corner seat, her back straight against the wall of the train, her knees bent and feet on the seat next to hers. Her eyes were closed. Qimmy did not call out to her, but she began to walk in the light dancing step Maria had described. She looked as if she were skipping on tiptoe, hands held at her shoulders like a toddler taking her first steps. Opal's eyes opened like window shades suddenly sprung to the top of their frame. Her unblinking eyes did not register any emotion, but her mouth pursed slightly to prevent the escape of some combination of relief and, I imagined, anger, as she might have felt our visit to be an intrusion. She swung her feet off the seat. Qimmy stationed herself between Opal's knees. I took the seat next to Opal.

"Can't take care of no walking babies," her low voice said into the top of Qimmy's hat. "Little babies, that's all."

"Okay. Just little babies," I agreed breathlessly. I was winded from our chase. We sat in silence, the train noisily proceeding on its uptown route. Qimmy, on her knees on the opposite seat, looking out the window, seemed mesmerized by the flash of tunnel lighting as we whizzed by. "I'm sorry we woke you," I said after a while. "Qimmy was asking for you and we were all worried about you, so we decided to take a chance on finding you here." Opal seemed unable to take in all of this concern. She responded to the first part of my message.

"I always ride with my eyes closed. More relaxing."

"How do you know when you get to where you're going?" I asked, then immediately felt stupid. After all, she might not really be going anywhere. The heated trains might be more comfortable alternatives to the cold stations.

"Smell," she said immediately. "Qimmy knows, too. Know we be at 238th Street by the smell of baking." There was a Stella D'oro factory a few blocks from there. "168th smell like mildew 'cause it's so far down, always damp. All them smell some kind of way." I sat in surprised silence. She was so much more talkative here. I remembered Mrs. Martin's message.

"I have a message for you from Queeny Martin. She wants

you to stay with her and Qimmy over Christmas. Kevin is going
down South for the holiday." A flicker of emotion shone on
Opal's face, then was gone. She gave no other response. "You can
talk to her about it when you see her," I suggested. Opal nodded.
I realized we had gone far uptown. We were just about to stop at
157th Street.

"Let's take Qimmy back to school," I said. Opal stood up
abruptly, took Qimmy's hand, and led her off the train, with me
sprinting to keep up with them as we moved to the other side of
the station where the downtown trains ran.

■　■　■

Franny and I got to the Salvation Army early. We wanted to make
the pre-Christmas group session festive, so we had planned a
cookie-baking project with the kids. We needed to arrive with
enough time to open up the kitchen and get the baking supplies
ready. The janitor met us at the door to lift the heavy metal gates.
The lobby, usually a sterile-looking open space with wooden
benches, was filled with Christmas accessories. Santa suits, money
collecting plates, and large bells were pushed over to one corner.
Children's shepherd costumes for the Christmas play covered the
wooden benches. An upset carton of homemade shepherds' staffs
wrapped in crepe paper and tied in place with tinsel bows littered
our path. When we flicked on the light switch, Christmas music
began filling the hallways. Franny and I smiled at each other. This
off-site location did have certain benefits. Probably the women
from the Home League would come in to bake Christmas pies
and fruitcakes later in the morning and offer us their leftovers.
We each tended to our preparations quietly, letting our own
private Christmas associations occupy us as we set out cookie
cutters and rolling pins, filling paper bowls with raisins, M&Ms,
cranberries, and popcorn. These pre-Christmas rituals transported Franny back to scenes from her Catholic childhood and
took me into a magical forbidden territory which Jewish children
must watch from afar. We were far away from each other when the
children pelted into the room, charged with anxious excitement.

"Where's the cookies?" demanded 'Mitri.

"You stupid crackhead!" Raquel admonished. "First we
gotta make 'em." 'Mitri stood frozen for a moment, as if para-

lyzed by hurt feelings, which any moment might be dissipated in a flare of defensive fury.

"What does that mean, Raquel? What you called 'Mitri? Because it looks like you hurt her feelings." I sought eye contact with Raquel, which she avoided.

"Mean she don't pay no attention to nothing," explained Raquel as she removed her boots.

"Unh-uh," countered Maimai. "Means she smoking crack and she feeling good." Maimai looked skyward with an exaggerated silly smile on her face.

Large tears began to fall from 'Mitri's large eyes. Franny moved to put her arm around 'Mitri's shoulder.

"We know 'Mitri isn't smoking crack, but maybe some of the grown-ups that she cares about might, and maybe some grown-ups that you care about, too." Raquel looked at me as if oblivious to the comment. Maimai went into an instant pout. Then she said, "Hey, let's play house, y'all."

"When we're going to make the cookies, then?" Angie asked with concern. Angie was always interested in cooking and eating. She ate chalk and paste at school when food was inaccessible.

"I know," said Maimai. "We can make the cookies and play house, too. We can all be mommies and daughters."

"I'm going to be Auntie," said Kendra decidedly.

"I be Grandmama," said 'Mitri, now recovered.

"I'm the mommy and Angie is my baby," Raquel added. Angie picked up a baby bottle and smiled. With that settled, all gathered at the round table and for a while remained absorbed in the pleasure of poking and patting the floury dough, sending clouds of flour into the air which settled like snowflakes on their braids and eyelashes. Maimai cut ten Santa faces in a row, then dropped the cookie cutter, dramatizing her final production and brushing her hands off noisily.

"Okay, y'all. Now play!" Maimai ordered. "Look! Look!" she shouted, looking at Kendra for confirmation. *"There* he go. That son of a bitch ain't coming in this house with that shit. Let him keep his crack-selling self out in the street."

"Don't curse!" said Raquel, distressed. "Don't curse 'cause the baby's listening."

"Where?" demanded Maimai, both hands on her hips. Raquel pointed at Angie, who was kneeling on the floor patting her play dough on the tabletop. "Oh," said Maimai, lowering her voice. "I ain't giving that bastard nothing, if you know what I mean," she whispered. "I ain't scared of him, neither." Kendra looked very uncomfortable.

"But he's strong, he might hurt you."

"So?" shrugged Maimai, reinvolving herself with the play dough. "Nothing hurts me anymore. My baby neither," she added, patting Angie's hand. There was silence for a while as each decorated her cookie cutouts with colored sprinkles and icing, eating large amounts of the ingredients as they worked. Finally the cookies were ready to be put in the oven. Everyone joined the procession to the kitchen, awestruck by their creations.

"They're going to be real pretty," said Raquel with satisfaction.

"*Now* what we going to do?" asked 'Mitri, throwing up her hands.

"Well," I said, "we have to wait ten minutes for the cookies to be done."

"I know. We'll have a meetin'," Maimai said emphatically. "Everyone get your chair and put it in a big circle." Franny and I looked at each other as they immediately complied. It usually took us twenty minutes of protest and fighting to accomplish the same thing. Maimai's eyes sparkled as she captured the group's attention. "We all gonna talk about something scary." Angie and Raquel wriggled with excitement, while Kendra looked at me for reassurance and 'Mitri's eyes glazed over.

"What scary thing do you want to talk about, Maimai?" I asked her.

"Something that happened to us last night," Maimai said with wide eyes. Maimai often included the group in her fantasies, and they were usually vivid enough to invite the others to buy into the collective theme. "Late last night, when we be trying to sleep, they be all kinds of noises, screaming and everything," began Maimai. "That's 'cause of the man wearing blood coming into the building from the walls and everywhere. Didn't ring the buzzer and ain't no one let him in, but he can climb in, don't need no key or nothing, trying to kill all the kids like Freddy Kruger. That's what I want to talk about." Maimai's face now lost its glow and she looked tense and fragile. No one spoke. Angie was rocking back and forth to comfort herself. I intervened.

"Maimai said she wanted to talk about something that happened to everyone. Does anyone else want to tell what they remember about last night?"

"I ain't seen Freddy last night," Raquel said timidly.

"What about the rest of you?" Franny asked 'Mitri and Angie and Kendra. They nodded their heads.

"You know what I think?" I said. "I think the stories we have been reading about Santa Claus have been scaring you because Santa wears a red suit like the scary man in Maimai's story and comes into the house without a key or a buzzer to let him in. I think the Santa Claus story is reminding you of times when people came in and you weren't safe."

"That's how it is where we live," Kendra said simply.

"Yeah," Maimai agreed, her face sagging with relief from the anxiety she felt before telling us about her fear. "That's how things be on our block."

■   ■   ■

There are times when listening to their hurt is too hard. There are times when poverty and pain surround the clinician and entangle her, so that she is unable to escape via the usual means of delineating "we" from "they." These can be times of therapeutic opportunity for the therapist, who then is forced to claim her own inner poverty and inner pain, instead of maintaining them in the distant "other." But sometimes the permission to feel the feelings that the work engenders comes when there is a break, and thus a disruption in the therapeutic support chain, a vacation from patients but also from the clinician's supervisors or her own analysis. The single therapist is thrown into the lap of friends and family in faraway places—people who have not invited the images of despair that may come along for the trip. Family members are never eager to know about the ways in which they might have contributed to their child's identification with deprivation, so it always seems better to plan the family visit after a vacation that truly involves relaxation in neutral territory.

For me, the territory was Puerto Rico, a place I had wanted to visit for some time. My work with Puerto Rican children and families who lived in New York always made me curious about the island. My friend Terry and I rented a car and drove into the mountains to one of the *paradores,* an old coffee plantation turned guest house. We unpacked, then sat on caned rocking chairs on a second-story porch, surrounded by giant leafy trees and jungly vines, and the sweet sounds of the Quoqui frogs. We sat overlooking the hills and valleys and tiny towns that we had driven through. The waiter came and took our order for piña coladas, which we drank in tall, freezing glasses topped with cherries. The warm sun melted the drinks faster than we could drink them, and the lush environment absorbed my urban images faster than I could let go of them. I imaged Opal allowing sleep only on the subway car, where she seemed to feel less endangered, perhaps because she was mobile and therefore not a helpless child behind the bars of her crib, a witness to and potential victim of murder. This image softened to become a hobo's lullaby image of Opal being rocked to sleep by the rhythm of the train. I imaged Maimai's invasive Santa fantasy born of her own treacherous associations with unwanted visitors. This image became an infant Maimai in a fleecy lined cradle, a black Santa filling her stocking with toys and food as she slept peacefully. Since I was on vacation, I sat still, content to allow the images to soften.

■ ■ ■

Ronnie looked beautiful in a new Irish sweater she had gotten for Hanukkah from Sara. It must have been important to her that I see it, because my building, like most New York prewar buildings, was extremely overheated. Ronnie spoke over the clanking of the steam radiator. "The whole staff of the school newspaper had the greatest Christmas party. Sara let me have it at my house." She was bubbling today. "Also my friend Marcia Allen says that Randy Reyes wanted to come to the party." She giggled.

"Did you want Randy Reyes to come?" I inquired. She shrugged.

"I don't know. He's not even on the paper, but he's okay." She reached for the magnet toy and began sculpting. "I'm really good in art," she said. "In school we're sculpting with papier-mâché. I'm making a contour map of Central America. You want to see it when it's finished?" she asked hurriedly.

"Sure, if you'd like me to." She busied herself with the sculpting for a few moments, creating a hollow hilly wall on the border of a round base. "I keep having dreams. They're scaring me," she said quietly.

"Tell me."

"Well, last night I had that one about the subway, but there was this woman in it." Ronnie shuddered.

"Tell me what the woman was like. You looked really scared when you told me she was there just now."

"Like the witch in *Snow White,* only old and wrapped up in this black sheet. Like, like the Ghost of Christmas Past in the movie *A Christmas Carol.* You can't see her face. She was just sitting there, but somehow she was in my way." Ronnie was animated by recalling her dream.

"Where were you going?"

"I don't know. Someplace on the train, I guess. But then I heard the beep and the same train came with those eyes, and they turned into black mirrors just like the last time. But this time I'm *in* them, and then I woke up and I was all sweaty." She shuddered again. "I keep trying to stay up really late because I want to be so tired that I'll just sleep like a stone and won't remember, and Sara wonders why all of a sudden I'm up so late at night."

"You didn't tell Sara you're having bad dreams?"

Ronnie shook her head.

"No," she said vehemently.

"How come?"

She shrugged. Then, "You won't tell her, will you?" she asked with panic in her voice.

"It's up to you to tell her if you want to. I just wondered why you don't want to."

"I just don't," she said with defiance. This was interesting; the first evidence of an adolescent transference between us coming up in defense of an idealized Sara. She seemed anxious to relieve Sara of any responsibility for her wakefulness. I said nothing and we were silent for a moment. "I mean, it's only a dream. It's not like someone's really hurting me. There's nothing Sara can do about it." Ronnie was looking more uncomfortable by the minute, frantic in her need to protect Sara, but now anxious that she might have offended me in the process.

"Well, it may be that nobody's hurting you in real life, but it looks like something's hurting you inside. You don't have to tell Sara, but I think it's really important that you do remember the dreams so that we can talk about them."

"You mean they're like clues to what's going on inside of me that's making me afraid?"

I nodded.

"But I don't understand the dreams. I don't know what they mean."

"But you know they make you feel scared, right?" I looked at her eyes, which were suddenly tearful. She looked back at me through the tears and nodded.

■   ■   ■

Betsy was jubilant. "Kevin decided to stay down South indefinitely. Opal's been at the Martins' place since Christmas Eve." She was whispering to me behind the cubby holes, in case Opal could hear us talking from the infant room. "Opal's still coming every day," she continued, with pride in her voice. "Even though she could just stay in Queeny's apartment. I think she really must like it here. We talked about the incident with Peter and agreed that if someone asked her to help with toddlers or older children, she would tell them that I said no."

"Good," I said, less than enthusiastically.

"You sound overjoyed," Betsy said. "What's the matter?"

"Sorry, it's just that Qimmy is an older child, as Opal would say, 'a walking baby.' Somehow we have to help her be able to let Qimmy act her age without Opal becoming unglued. Otherwise, how are we going to make a positive recommendation to Franklyn in the event that they get the Martins' apartment, which, by the way, is still anyone's guess. I've called Housing about twenty-five times and I'm still getting the runaround."

"I'll leave those projects to you and Franklyn," Betsy said, gathering sheets from the cubbyholes to put in the wash. "I'll be in charge of day care for mother and child; you do the rest."

"Considering you didn't want to get involved at all, you're really something." I grinned at her and she grinned back.

"Yeah, I know," she agreed heartily. "I know."

I brought Qimmy back to her miniature subway scene, which I had asked Betsy to leave standing with her name card taped to it. "That's where you and I went," I said to her. "That's like the station where you and I went to find Mommy before Christmas." Qimmy squinted at me as though trying to recall. Then she squatted down near the toys and pulled the train through the tunnel, first one way and then the other. This play seemed very comforting to her, and she rested her head on one knee and got a sleepy look in her eyes as she repeated it. "Now, how about some people?" I suggested. "I'm going to find a baby Qimmy, a Mommy Opal, and then there's all the other people that you made waiting for the train." I put the baby and the mommy dolls in the open palm of her free hand. Qimmy looked at me sideways. For a moment I thought she might dance away from me, but she did not. Instead, she bent the mommy doll so that it was in a sitting position and sat it on the block-turned-bench. The baby was placed some inches away, within the mommy's sight but not reach, and facing the people. I decided to have the people become animated. "Look at the people, baby. They are walking to the train and some are walking to the street. They've all passed by the mommy and the baby." I moved as many little people back and forth as I could manage. Qimmy became animated also. She looked at me with a look I read as surprise, then began dancing the baby back and forth between the sitting mother and the moving people. "What's the baby doing, Qimmy?" I asked.

"Juice," I heard her say.

"Juice? What do you mean?" I couldn't make sense of this right away, but Qimmy did not repeat it. Hmm. Opal had said that Qimmy wandered off in the station, and I had seen her do that when we visited Opal. Opal needed Qimmy to stay an infant: a milk-drinking lap baby. But Qimmy had learned to walk and needed more than milk. Although to our knowledge Opal didn't panhandle, Qimmy might have. Her dancing Tinkerbell eyes might have been her best survival tool, her means of engaging

people just long enough to announce her existence, in itself a
plea for sustenance. And very likely Qimmy's face was either shut
out by passersby who could not tolerate the pain of seeing a
toddler in need, or was occasionally answered by a cookie or
container of juice. Qimmy wandered off, but maybe there was
something else that she was doing. Maybe she was creating a
bridge between Opal and the rest of humanity, staying connected
to Opal in some way but also reaching out for what she needed.

I translated my theory into practice. I went to get some tiny
plastic food from the dollhouse toy shelf. "Look, Qimmy! Juice.
Juice for the baby." A lady held the juice out and Qimmy made
the baby doll dance over and claim it. She looked very satisfied
with this outcome, then sprang to her feet and skipped away,
leaving me with the juice-drinking baby. I followed her with my
eyes. I watched her seat herself for apple juice and crackers,
swinging her feet under the table and looking at the ceiling as she
munched. It occurred to me that what looked like Qimmy's non-
chalance—her dancing away—was really her distancing herself
from her own emotional hunger, which if felt might have rendered her at risk of starvation, potentially lifeless. Qimmy's dance
was a dance for life.

■   ■   ■

I was using the phone at the clinic during my lunch hour. "Housing," they answered.

"Hi. I'm calling on behalf of an elderly tenant in the Douglas
housing project. She is sharing her apartment with a mother and
child who would otherwise be homeless. The mother is on the
Douglas waiting list and qualifies as homeless and therefore eligible for the project. The tenant is interested in knowing what, if
any, claim her housemate may have on the apartment in the event
of her death."

"The housemate would have to go through the regular chan-
nels, ma'am."

"Yes, but she may be homeless again by the time her name
comes up on the list."

"Ma'am, Public Housing currently has a waiting list of two
hundred thousand. Many of those people are homeless and
therefore priority cases. Has this woman stayed at a tier-two shel-

ter for the prescribed period, and has her case been transferred to a welfare hotel?"

"No. She's unable to stay in shelters for the prescribed period. She has psychiatric problems for which she receives SSI."

"Well, if she's unable to stay in the shelter without assistance, she can receive assistance from our special problems unit once inside the shelter."

"Yes, I believe she received that service once before but it was insufficient. That's why we are so eager to facilitate her receipt of the apartment that may become available."

"I'm sorry, ma'am. What you're asking is impossible. If she's on the waiting list, she's done all that she can do. Call us again if you need further assistance." Click. Dial tone. My fingers waited some minutes, hoping that a different operator would answer the phone this time.

"Housing."

"Hi. I'm calling on behalf of an elderly tenant in the Douglas housing project. She is sharing her apartment with her daughter and granddaughter, who would otherwise be homeless. She's anxious to know whether her daughter has a claim on the apartment in the event of her death."

"Who's name is on the lease?"

"The tenant's name."

"Just the tenant's name?"

"Yes, I believe just the tenant's name."

"One moment, please." I ate my cheese sandwich and recorded my notes from the session for several minutes. "Ma'am?"

"Yes."

"The tenant would have to reapply to include her daughter's name on the lease. Her daughter would need to qualify as well. It would be the city's prerogative to approve or deny the request."

"Based on what?"

"Their own assessment criteria, ma'am."

"Yes, I understand. But what constitutes the criteria?"

"I'm sorry, we are unable to give that information over the telephone. In the event that the tenant applies and is rejected, the tenant would then request an appointment to discuss unmet criteria."

Great! I thought. By that time the tenant may be dead.

"Thank you," I said, and hung up.

Hmm. It wasn't completely clear to me, but it did seem that a relative had more of a shot at the apartment. In that case, I guessed it was worth pursuing Plan B. I called Franklyn.

"Guess what?" I asked him.

"Opal States is currently residing with Mrs. Martin and Qimmy."

"Who told you?"

"Queeny Martin called, which I asked her to do, to report any changes."

"Great."

"Now here's the story. I called Housing and it seems there is a chance that Opal would get the apartment if she were Queeny's daughter. So . . ."

"So you are going to rewrite history."

"No. So I think Queeny should try to adopt Opal."

Silence.

"I don't know. That sounds like . . . I don't know. I suppose she could become Opal's guardian, but then Opal would have to be declared incompetent. But then she couldn't sign a lease if she were incompetent. I don't know. The adoption of adults . . . it's never come up before. It really strikes me as a shot in the dark. Shit, I'm not even convinced that Opal can handle Qimmy on her own if they did get the apartment. Why don't you just be satisfied that Opal's in somebody's house and out of the cold? You can't solve everything for everyone, you know."

I ignored his negative attitude. "Well, what about with Preventive Services—like a homemaker, for instance? I think that Opal could provide care for Qimmy with Preventive Services, and she could get it because of her psychiatric disability."

"Possibly," said Franklyn, mulling it over. "We'll cross that bridge if and when we come to it."

"Meanwhile, doesn't C.W.A. have lawyers who can look into this adoption thing?"

Franklyn sighed. "All right, I'll look into the adoption thing. Just don't hold your breath, okay?"

"Me? Certainly not," I countered. "But try to find out fast.

It strikes me as the kind of procedure that could take a long time."

"Sure thing," Franklyn teased, "no problem. I have nothing else to do all day other than work on the States case every minute."

"Good," I said cheerfully. "Bye!"

■ ■ ■

"We thought you were dead," said Maimai, eyes wide with betrayal. 'Mitri and Angie nodded in tandem.

"Y'all shouldn't be scaring us that way," scolded Raquel, her arms folded across her chest.

We were in the elevator, having met the bus downstairs, since the walkway was icy. There had been a snow day the first day after vacation when the group was supposed to meet, and most of the kids could not be notified, as the families had no phones.

"It really scared you when the bus didn't come on Monday," I remarked, hugging Angie and Maimai as we rode up. Raquel and 'Mitri immediately moved over to be hugged by Franny. Kendra was standing alone, clutching her book bag to her chest and looking at the numbers lighting up on the elevator panel.

"My mommy knew," said Raquel proudly. Raquel's family had a telephone. "She went to Kendra's house and told Kendra's auntie." Kendra continued looking at the numbers and saying nothing.

"Shit," said Maimai dramatically as we unlocked the room and they burst in, "I even peed on myself I was so worried about y'all." This was an amazing connection for Maimai to make. She almost never referred to her accidents.

"Do you remember how you were feeling before that happened?" I asked her. "If you thought we were dead, maybe you were feeling very sad."

"I wasn't crying," countered Maimai, "just thinking about ya'll being dead and never coming back, and the pee come out." She picked up her juice bottle and popped it into her mouth.

"Maybe it was too scary to feel about us being dead, so maybe you had to find a way to let your feelings out before you felt them, so you peed."

"Your mommy beat your butt?" inquired 'Mitri with interest and sadistic excitement.

"She don't do that no more." Maimai shook her head, look-ing at me as she said it. This was a hopeful sign if true.

"What did other people think about what happened on Monday?" Franny asked.

"Maybe you left on an airplane, and you got to Puerto Rico and it was *bien bonita* and you said, 'Let me stay here.' So . . ." Angie was jumping up and down holding one of Franny's hands. This had probably been her experience with various relatives who went back and forth between Puerto Rico and the mainland.

"What about you, Kendra?" I asked her.

Kendra shrugged. Her face was sullen and brittle-looking and her eyes were angry.

"She ain't saying nothin' this morning," reported Raquel. "She wouldn't say good mornin' or nothin' to the bus driver this mornin'. Her auntie smack her."

Oh. This was probably a rare experience for Kendra, who tried so hard not to offend anyone.

"Kendra will talk to us when she's ready," Franny offered.

"Come here," demanded 'Mitri, grabbing my hand and pull-ing me to the book corner. "Read this one." She chose the story *You Go Away* followed by *The Runaway Bunny,* two books about comings and goings which we would often read to the kids when they were anxious about separation. It helped them to hear their feelings reflected in the stories, to know that these were issues that could be shared and given form. The children all skipped over to the rug, cuddling on laps and pillows, pushing and complaining about not being able to see. All except Kendra, who stood at the easel, painting.

" 'If you are a sailboat,' said the mommy to the bunny," I read, " 'I will be the wind and I will blow you home.' "

Splat! We all looked up to see a paint container that Kendra had hurled into the air splatter against the wall and then drip down to stain Maimai's favorite baby doll with a thick blob of red paint. Maimai gasped and hid her face in her pillow. I jumped up to get Kendra, who had already dissolved into high-pitched, piercing sobs. The other children miraculously stayed with Franny, allowing me to tend to Kendra without disruption.

I sat on the floor behind her and held her as she sobbed. She was hard to hold, not because she struggled, but because sexual abuse had made touching dangerous for her and tenderness hard to receive. For many minutes she sat wailing, leaning against me, shutting her eyes against my presence, leaving herself alone with the pain. Finally the sobs subsided and she lay down with her head in my lap, her eyes open.

"You said," she hiccuped, "you said you were comin' back Monday and . . ."

"And I didn't," I said for her, "and you felt so sad and so worried." The group was her safety net and it hadn't felt safe.

She nodded, then cried for a few more seconds. Then she shut her eyes and closed her fingers around my thumb and held it very tightly.

■   ■   ■

I received a call from Ronnie's guidance counselor. He thought Ronnie might be "doing something."

"Doing something?" I inquired.

Maybe smoking pot, he said. Ronnie didn't seem to be high, but her eyes looked red. She was always sleepy at school.

I thanked him for the call and said I didn't think we had to worry about pot, but that Ronnie might be having difficulty sleeping. He hung up, much relieved.

"I got a call from your counselor at school," I began, when Ronnie and I next met. She froze for a moment, blue eyes fixed intently on my mouth, trying to lip-read the next words before I spoke them. "He was worried because you looked so sleepy."

Ronnie let her breath out and her earrings went back to their usual soft jangling. "For a minute I thought you were going to say that he told you I couldn't come back," she blurted.

"Why would he do that?" I wondered.

Ronnie shrugged. "Maybe my grades aren't high enough or something."

This didn't make any sense. Ronnie was getting A's, even at home.

"Have your grades been falling since you've gone back to school?" Might be the lack of sleep, I thought.

"Well, I don't think so. We didn't get our report cards yet."

Silence.

"Anyway, Mr. Weston already asked me why I look sleepy. I guess he didn't believe me."

"What did you tell him?"

"That my neighbors were making too much noise and I couldn't sleep."

"Hmm," I said, looking at her.

"Well, the whole world doesn't have to know I'm crazy," she said bitterly. The tone startled me. I had never heard this in her voice before.

"You sound really angry about needing to come here," I said.

"You didn't tell him about the dreams, did you?" she asked anxiously, skipping over my interpretation completely.

"Nope, just that you weren't sleeping well. He thought you might be smoking pot."

Ronnie covered her mouth with her hand, stifling a burst of anxious laughter. "Me?" she squealed. "That sounds more like Sara when she was a teenager." She smiled with delight at this mistaken conclusion.

"Does Sara tell you a lot of stories about when she was your age?"

"Hmm." Ronnie looked thoughtful. "More about when she was older and she was already in the Peace Corps. I think that was her happiest time," she said wistfully, as if she were recalling her own experiences. "She met my dad in the Peace Corps, you know."

"I know. Sara told me. Do you and your mom ever talk about him?"

"No, I guess she doesn't like to. But my grandma talks about him sometimes. She says, 'Your daddy must be a good man, *Mamaleh,* to start out in life taking care of other people instead of being busy making money for himself.' That's how my grandma talks." She yawned as if to put that topic to bed, then stretched her legs out straight in front of her and clasped her hands over her stomach. "I'm tired," she complained. "My friend's mother said maybe I could get sleeping pills." She looked at me with a winning expression.

"I don't think you need sleeping pills. I think you need to

talk some more about the dreams and why they are so scary you don't want to sleep."

"I *told* you already," she said, exasperated. "The subway dreams are scary because of those eyes."

"What's so scary about the eyes?" I pursued her.

"I'm *in* them. God! How would you like to see yourself inside somebody else's eyes?" she asked angrily.

I thought about this. Seeing yourself reflected in someone else's eyes was one of those romantic or maternal images found in poetry or song lyrics, not ghost stories.

"I guess you don't like seeing yourself inside someone else's eyes," I commented.

"And that lady without the face keeps coming up in my other dreams, too." She sat fighting her tears.

"Tell me about the other dreams," I said softly. "What does she do in the other dreams?"

"She just sits there . . . looking . . . scary, like . . . she wants to . . ." She sniffled.

"Wants to what?"

". . . Make me disappear or something." She wiped the tears with the back of her hand. "Am I crazy?" she asked suddenly.

Everybody's favorite question.

"Are you crazy because you have bad dreams?" I asked.

She shook her head. "Because I am so scared," she said, crying again.

"It's not crazy to feel scared," I answered gently. "It might *feel* pretty crazy, though, to feel so much fear all of a sudden."

"That's what I heard Sara say to a friend on the phone. She said, 'All of a sudden, Ronnie is afraid of her own shadow.' I was thinking, boy, is Sara smart, because the lady in the dream is just like that—a big scary shadow that looks at you without eyes, and then you're captured by her and you're a shadow, too. It's just like that," Ronnie said with some relief. "It's just like that."

■　■　■

I was eating something that Tina's mother had made. It had an Italian name but tasted like Jewish "kuchen."

"I think Ronnie's 'shadow woman' is really her impression of homeless women in the subway. When she was telling me the

dream about the faceless woman I started thinking about Opal,"
I said between bites.

Tina was fascinated by this theory. "You don't think it could
actually *be* Opal. . . ."

"No, wrong stop."

She smiled and sipped her coffee.

"Why . . . ?" we both said simultaneously. "It must be Sara,"
we continued together.

Tina giggled. "This is ridiculous. Does it make sense to you?"

"Not really," I confessed. "There's not enough to go on. Sara
idealizes Ronnie's infancy and gets furious with me if I even imply
that she might have had power struggles as a toddler. The denial
of Ronnie's need to be oppositional may be a clue to Sara's
feelings about Ronnie's adolescent need to separate, but where is
the 'shadow woman' in all this? I don't know."

"Well, sometimes idealized periods turn out to be less than
ideal. Who cared for Ronnie when Sara was working and they
lived in Peru? Maybe someone who wasn't quite all there, whose
eyes and mind were elsewhere. I don't know. Be a detective," Tina
ordered.

I nodded, accepting this mission. "Meanwhile, Sara's mother
provides Ronnie with a positive image of her father. She tells
Ronnie he's a good man because he takes care of people, but no
one tells Ronnie that her dad sends money to take care of her!"
I told Tina about Ronnie's asking if she was crazy. "She's not
crazy," I mused, "only confused about where her fears lie. She's
afraid to go outside even though her fears are on the inside. Opal,
on the other hand, is afraid for her life. For her, danger is everywhere. She can't risk being trapped in a house with it, so she
either has to play dead or take refuge in something mobile so that
at least she becomes a moving target. She has survived situations
that would have finished most of us off. *She* qualifies as crazy, but
what she does is not so crazy, considering."

"Nothing is crazy, considering. The difference is that Ronnie
can articulate her pain and Opal has lost touch with her own
emotional voice. She has isolated her feelings for so long. The
silence may be impenetrable at this point," Tina hypothesized
sadly. "Maybe that's the scary part."

"Maybe," I agreed, "but what about Qimmy?"

"I don't know. The choices aren't great. You can help Opal with the housing needs, get Preventive Services to keep the case, and hope for the best, with foster care as a backup plan. Or you can try to work with Opal and risk her getting flooded with emotion and becoming less functional than she is now or—"

"Never mind. I don't think I want to deal with any other inspiring options at the moment, thank you."

"You're welcome," Tina said.

■ ■ ■

We decided that the Child Care Center was not the place to do mother-child work with Opal and Qimmy. Opal felt deprived by any time away from the infant room. Her contact with the infants was sacred to her. When a baby lay in her arms she seemed to melt. Her face looked soft and round, and her body molded itself around the infant. When the babies were otherwise occupied, Opal would sit motionless and seconds later would appear unrecognizable as a nurturer, her chiseled face and leaden body taking over. Qimmy could not compete with the pull that the babies had for Opal, no matter how infantile Qimmy's behavior might be.

I was beginning to wonder if Qimmy was being neglected because of our efforts to help Opal, so we decided I would make home visits to Mrs. Martin's apartment and do some work with Qimmy and Opal there. This idea seemed to have many advantages. Mrs. Martin could be present as a support to Opal, the work would be done in the home environment and so would hopefully be more easily internalized as part of the family repertoire, and I would have the opportunity to observe Opal and Qimmy at home, which appealed to Franklyn. On the negative side, the apartment was tiny, there was a lack of play space and a lack of age-appropriate toys for Qimmy, and I felt concerned about intruding on Mrs. Martin, despite her assurance that I was welcome.

I rang the bell and heard sounds of straightening up and then the sound of Mrs. Martin opening the several locks. She smiled and her head trembling slightly, gestured for me to enter. Qimmy was skipping around the room, apparently excited by the visit. Opal sat in a plastic-covered armchair in the corner, her hands curled over the edges of the wooden arms; she lifted one finger in greeting. I looked at her for moment, now sheltered, dressed in a combination of Mrs. Martin's spare clothes and her own garments, clean and dry, no scarf tied around her Afro, which now framed her face with a hint of softness. As before, the heaviness of her presence remained. When I saw her seated this way, it was difficult to imagine that she would ever move from the spot.

The agenda today was the adoption. Having a set agenda made it less awkward. It was as though I had a specific mission and I came by to carry it out. It indeed appeared possible for Mrs. Martin to adopt Opal. However, this might necessitate Opal's making a court appearance, and we did not know if Opal would be willing to do this. Mrs. Martin and I sat down on the sofa, Mrs. Martin squeezing herself over to the corner to be closer to Opal.

"Opal." Mrs. Martin took a deep breath and then began, her voice trembling with age and emotion. "I'd be real pleased if you let me adopt you. After all, I've been like a mama to you once. My own daughter is so far away, you know." Mrs. Martin's daughter taught in the Virgin Islands. "And y'all would have a better chance of keeping this apartment when I go to the Lord. So, all in all, I think it'd be a real good idea and I be pleased if you'd agree." She stopped to catch her breath and push her glasses up on her nose. Opal squinted at her uncomprehendingly. Qimmy felt the solemn mood of the moment and stopped jumping. Resisting the temptation to rush in with further explanations that would break the tension, I held on to my words. Finally Opal spoke.

"Too late for that, I guess. I ain't no child." She glanced at me suspiciously, and I wondered whether she thought we were trying to have her declared incompetent.

"No, you're an adult," I said. "But it's legal for one adult to adopt another. The reason we thought about this is because Mrs. Martin wants you and Qimmy to have this apartment, but we checked it out and you don't have any right to it if you're not related. Well, that is, you might have a right to it in the long run, but it wouldn't be guaranteed. If you get adopted, you would have a better chance. Then Mrs. Martin can apply to include you on the lease." Opal relaxed a little. She let out her breath, which she had been holding. She pursed her lips the way she did when she was afraid feelings might escape without her permission.

"May have to go to court once or twice, take care of all the legal ramifications," Mrs. Martin explained. "My late husband's friend, Mr. Willie Trevor, is an attorney. He'd be more than happy to do this piece of work for me. He'd be more than happy." I smiled in admiration. Mrs. Martin was a woman of many resources.

"Qimmy be your grandbaby then?" Opal asked suddenly.

"Guess she would be," Mrs. Martin replied thoughtfully. "Guess she would be. That's only right since she's named for me, isn't that so?" Opal nodded. Her mouth was still pursed, but her eyes were smiling. Mrs. Martin patted Opal's hand, which was still holding the arm of the chair. "Well, that's just fine then. Just fine. I'll call Mr. Trevor soon as we get finished here."

I decided I'd better clarify my role in all this. "You know, if all of this works out we're still going to have to convince Franklyn that Opal can take proper care of Qimmy, and that might not be so easy because you're great at taking care of holding babies, but Qimmy's a walking child and you know how that can be." I addressed this last part to Opal by looking directly at her. She looked down in response. "So my idea is for all of us to meet here every other week or so and work on having Qimmy and you get to know more about being together. It's been a long, long time since the days when you had your own place." I stopped finally, feeling very intrusive. Opal looked up at Mrs. Martin, who had no qualms about influencing Opal during the moment of consent. She nodded decisively.

"I told Miss Lesley she was always a welcome visitor, any time."

Opal looked nervous for a minute, then her concern burst out. "Still be welcome at the day-care center, then?" she asked anxiously.

"Yes," I reassured. "That's between you and Betsy. It's not really related to anything we arrange."

"Okay, then," her low voice answered. "Okay, then."

Qimmy felt the tension break and began dancing around

between the adults, her full, flowered skirt twirling and creating a rainbow of color.

■   ■   ■

Sara had called requesting a telephone session in lieu of her regular appointment. She felt overwhelmed at work. I asked her about the various people who had cared for Ronnie when Ronnie was younger. Sara had had no difficulty with early child care for Ronnie. In Peru she had chosen a woman in the village who was warm with all babies and especially attracted to Ronnie. She had been intrigued by Ronnie's red hair and used to dress it with strings of wildflowers. Ronnie cooed and babbled in delight when they played together, and even learned to call the woman's name, Digna. When she got older and they returned to the States, Sara's mother, Rena, always provided baby-sitting when Sara needed it. They had lived in the same building in Brooklyn at the time, so it was not difficult for Sara to get Ronnie to her grandmother's house. How would Sara describe Ronnie's early relationship to her grandmother? I wondered.

"Ronnie was cherished by her grandmother, who was natural and loving with her," was Sara's answer. "Ronnie still calls her grandmother 'Mama,' and her grandmother calls Ronnie '*Mama-leh*' in Yiddish." Sara's mother was a Russian immigrant who had managed to escape before Hitler's occupation. She talked to Ronnie about her family sometimes, and Sara had been glad of that because she believed it stimulated Ronnie's political consciousness at an early age. Hmm. This gave me something to think about. I began to think about the shadow woman as perhaps representing the disenfranchised self of Sara's mother, forced to flee her homeland, and the self she left behind, buried in loss of friends and family. A homeless person could evoke this association. Governmental fathers were perhaps not persecuting the street people directly, but they were allowing them to be persecuted and neglected.

The question was, what did all of this mean to Ronnie? I looked forward to my next meeting with Ronnie because I felt we had a lot to explore. Ronnie apparently felt this way, too, because she entered with more enthusiasm than usual and found her agenda quickly.

"Let's draw," she said unexpectedly. Other than playing with the magnet sculpture, Ronnie had never used any of the play materials in the room. "Can I use that marker board?" she asked, pointing to a large white eraser board in the corner. "I told you I'm good at art," she commented, arranging herself at the board and then setting the markers out on the floor in front of her. I sat in a butterfly chair with my head leaning on my hands, watching Ronnie work. She was indeed good at art. The heavy, dry marker colors glided across the board in her hands, creating shades and shadow out of what were usually bright bold primary colors. "I'm drawing the dream I had last night," she said, and these were the last words she spoke for much of the session.

She was drawing a large pear-shaped figure filled in with concentric pear shapes of black, gray and purples, leaving a circular blank space in the middle of the small top part of the pear, another space almost in the center of the large bottom part. I moved to the floor for a better view. Ronnie was intently coloring in the two circular spaces with black. Her drawing looked something like a Russian doll but with an inner void and an obliterated face. Next came a much smaller and slighter pear shape, colored with long reddish-orange swirling lines, with some rich turquoise shading in between. Ronnie stopped for a second, one hand holding the back end of the marker to her mouth and the other holding the toe of her sneaker. She saw only the drawing and the dream inspiring it. Then she drew many lines, some vertical and some horizontal, some giving the impression of train tracks and some of underground pillars. Next she blackened all the white spaces, which took several minutes, as the board was quite large.

"I can see a lot of what you've been talking about here," I ventured. But there was no response; the only sound was the occasional squeak of the marker against the board. I looked away for a second, and when I looked back Ronnie's finger, rubbing away the dry marker, was creating two holes in the large shadow woman's stomach. These she colored bright yellow, then extended them like beams of light, boring through the woman's middle and toward the smaller figure. The light looked ominous, like something from *Star Wars*, like a powerful laser that could cause Ronnie to disappear. Ronnie let the marker roll from her hand and leaned back, just looking at her drawing for a moment.

"There," she said with great relief. "I finally drew it."

"Have you tried to draw it before?" I asked her with surprise. That was the first I had heard of it.

"A bunch of times in art class, but I can never do it. But I can do it here." She leaned back on both hands and looked very satisfied, tossing her red hair.

"Does drawing make it less scary for you?" I asked her.

"It makes it . . ." She looked up, thinking. "Like I designed the whole thing, you know? Like I have the power to make it appear and disappear." It was just about time for the session to end.

"So?" I said. "Are you going to make it disappear before you leave?" Ronnie shook her head and looked at me shyly.

"No, I'm leaving it here. You can look at it for a while." She smiled at this, picked up her knapsack and sailed out, leaving the shadow woman, the shadow child, and me quite alone.

■   ■   ■

"Let's play that we grow up," proposed Raquel loudly. They had each been in their own worlds today, unusually quiet, each involved in her own activity. This invitation startled them and then drew them to the house corner, where Raquel had been sitting, fixing her baby's hair.

"Well, what you gonna be then?" Kendra asked officiously.

"Hmm." Raquel sucked her fingers to think about it. "A nursie like my mommy," she said proudly. Raquel's mother was a nurse's aide in a local hospital.

"How 'bout you, Angie?" Kendra asked, pointing her finger at Angie's chubby belly.

"A mommy," Angie answered promptly. She alternated between play at being the mommy she needed and play at being the needy baby she still was.

"You crazy?" challenged 'Mitri. "You wanna change all those diapers and be spending all your time in line waitin' for your check?"

"I ain't gonna wait in line, 'Mitri," Angie said indignantly. "I'm going to tell them to put my check in the mailbox."

"Shoot," said 'Mitri. "I ain't playing with y'all. I don't wanna be no grown-up." She stomped away.

"Why?" Maimai called after her, standing very still and looking somewhat stricken.

"Crack, that's why, you stupid head." Crack was a good reason. 'Mitri had gone back to the train track that she had been assembling before Raquel's house idea. Maimai stood holding her baby doll, considering this. Franny and I awaited her response, as Maimai spent many group hours playing her version of grown-up, a very streetwise woman who seemed almost to possess Maimai and act through her body, animated by the release of the overwhelmingly adult images she stored without understanding. Maimai decided to focus her attention on the others.

"What you going to be, Kendra?" she demanded. Kendra was swinging herself by leaning one hand on the play sink and the other on the play table, then lifting her body from the ground and pumping her legs.

"A nun," Kendra said matter-of-factly.

"A nun!" screamed Maimai and Raquel simultaneously.

"That mean you gonna wear black dresses all the time, even when you're sleeping," warned Raquel.

"And you don't get to do no dancing or wear makeup neither," Maimai added.

Kendra shrugged. "My auntie says nuns are married to God, so they don't have no boyfriends and they don't have to . . . you know." Kendra had found a fantasy that helped her feel that growing up could be safe. Being deprived of certain advantages did not seem too high a price to pay.

"Ooh," said Maimai, giggling.

"I'm going to be married to God, too," Angie said with certainty, dressing up in play high heels and an oversized veiled hat as she spoke. The part about being married to God sounded good to Angie. She was always attracted by anything she thought might bring her closer to God, who kept her mother from her reach.

"No!" 'Mitri yelled frantically, a prisoner of reality. "You can't be no nun if you gonna have babies like you said you was gonna!"

Angie had been looking in the mirror at her reflection, altered by her dress-up costume. I glanced at her just in time to see her face contort a warning that she could not cope with an assault on her fantasy. Neither could she organize a verbal response quickly enough. I jumped up from where I had been eating pretend peas cooked by Raquel, but it was too late. Angie had lunged at 'Mitri and bitten her on the forearm. 'Mitri screamed in pain. I yanked Angie away before any retaliation was possible, and Franny sprang to 'Mitri's side to provide comfort and first aid. We would make interpretations later. 'Mitri's bite had to be cleaned and disinfected. Angie had to be sat apart. Biting was very serious business these days—the kids were at high risk for AIDS, and parents became very concerned if a child was bitten.

"Angie," I said to her pouting, sullen face as I sat her in a chair on the other side of the room, "you can't . . ."

She covered her ears, denial being her only reliable defense.

I continued, regardless: "You can't bite people. If you're angry you have to use angry words, and if you can't, you have to tell Franny or me to help you." I felt angry at her for disrupting what was going on as well as for hurting 'Mitri. She was kicking her feet against the floor in protest, making quite a racket.

"Stay there until I tell you you can get up," I told her in a firm voice.

'Mitri had left the room with Franny. Maimai was paralyzed with her baby in a corner on the floor. Her response to any emotional outburst, other than her own, was paralysis. Raquel was staring intently into her pot on the stove, which by now perhaps contained a mixture of all the raw emotions filling the room. Angie was sobbing.

Kendra came over to me, reaching up to touch the ends of my frizzy hair.

"Do nuns really have to wear black clothes to sleep?" she whimpered. Raquel's imagery had frightened her. I bent down and she came up onto my lap.

"Did Raquel scare you?" I asked her gently.

She nodded.

"I guess the idea of being a nun is a way you can think of to be a grown-up and still keep yourself safe, but the black dress at night doesn't sound very safe to you." Kendra listened, stroking my hair.

"But *do* they wear black clothes to sleep in?" she persisted.

I wasn't much of an expert on the sleeping attire of nuns. "Well, I never really saw a nun get ready to go to sleep, but I bet they wear nightgowns maybe like Auntie wears." Kendra's aunt was elderly. It seemed logical to me that a nun's nightdress would resemble an elderly aunt's.

"Good," said Kendra, much relieved. "Well, come on, Mai-mai, let's play grown-up." With some trepidation, Maimai walked her baby back into the house corner.

■ ■ ■

My plan was to leave the clinic by three-thirty, get to the day-care center by four-thirty to play with Qimmy, then meet my brother for dinner at six. To arrive on time I would have to take the subway down from the Bronx, then transfer to a crosstown bus at 96th Street, run the three blocks to the center, and hope for the best. But I was thwarted from the beginning. The number 4 train was running on the local track instead of the express, so the trip was taking twice as long as usual.

I sat squished between a large Latin woman with an ancient-looking face, who was transporting dozens of woven shawls in a giant paper shopping bag, and a tall man balancing a cello between his knees. I sat thinking about the inordinate number of New Yorkers who seemed to play the cello, an instrument not easily accommodated in crowded apartments or subway cars, just as an inordinate number of New Yorkers who inhabited tiny city dwellings had giant dogs. It was as though in the urban culture all empty spaces cried out to be filled. If a space was allowed to remain empty for too long, people became frightened, afraid of hearing their own inner emptiness echoing above the city's din.

My thoughts were interrupted at intervals by a series of women walking through the car, panhandling. Many were ema-ciated and ill-clad, with eyes glassy from illness or drugs. Passen-gers busied themselves with newspapers and paperbacks. Others bought their freedom from confrontation by reaching into their pockets. Unlike Opal, who seemed to shrink from contact when in need, these women were aggressively pursuing change. One woman with a crack addict's rotten teeth, skeletal frame, and shiny eyes insisted that each passenger at least acknowledge her pain by repeating "Excuse me" over and over as she stood in front of each person until his or her eyes met hers. I had run out of "Women in Need" referral slips and didn't want to give her the tokens that I would need later that day. I shook my head, but she did not move on right away. Instead, she leaned against the pole directly in front of me and delivered an icy stare that seemed as though it might have the power to evaporate its victim or transform her to an equally debilitated state. I shuddered as I left the train, feeling the weight of that stare as it might be borne by a thirteen-year-old girl, considering the pros and cons of growing up.

By the time I got to Qimmy, nap time was long over and the majority of the afternoon children who remained until six o'clock were milling about. This would make it difficult for me to engage Qimmy without constant interruption. Qimmy herself had been asleep and now sat at the snack table with untied shoelaces and sleepy eyes.

"Hi, Qimmy," I said, seating myself in the chair next to hers. To my surprise, she scrambled into my lap and buried her head in my nubby sweater. I was stunned—this had not been part of the Qimmy-Lesley repertoire. I sat holding her and she sat cuddling, her eyes closed and her long lashes brushing against my arm.

"Are you going to wake up so we can play?" I asked her, realizing as soon as I said it that this was a stupid thing to say. It seemed that the sleepy feeling pulled her back to the regressed and restful state of a premobile infant that Opal had nurtured so well. But for the majority of the day she had probably been the on-the-go Qimmy, Qimmy the forager, Qimmy the navigator, Qimmy who kept her distance and guarded her space, but functioned as if her survival depended upon her own stealing initiatives. My intrusion had forced her to jump over the gap that separated long ago from the present. She had reached for me and pulled me into her past for the first time. I rocked her for a while, no longer inclined to move her into a play session. The infant Qimmy, whose fist was now in her mouth, was the Qimmy we needed to get to know, the Qimmy we needed to begin with.

INTERIOR
DESIGNS

My brother and I sat waiting for egg drop soup. We often met at Chinese restaurants for a meal that was breakfast for Michael and dinner for me. I always arrived first and was seated, then tried to describe Michael with a combination of words and mime to the Chinese-speaking waitress. "Tall, thin, wild hair," I would mime. The waitress of the evening would nod and smile, and fifteen minutes later proudly produce Michael from the line of people waiting. "He look like you," she would comment.

We smiled at this. Actually, Michael looked like our mother and I looked like our father. Then again, there were the hair and eyebrows—in that way, our entire family looked alike.

"What's new?" Michael always began. We were both storytellers, but Michael's stories were usually longer and more dramatic, better suited as the main feature, while I provided the previews and the after-dinner commentary.

"Not enough," I answered, waiting for the waitress to finish arranging the soup and fried noodles on our tiny table. This question was really a code for "Have you met anyone recently?"

"Just psychiatrists and doormen," I elaborated. These were

the two categories of men that I had contact with on a daily basis. Neither group had proved promising so far.

Michael would have had little opportunity for contact with either of these groups. He was a musician, living a nocturnal life-style, playing in clubs at night and in the park on summer weekends. He lived in a walk-up apartment with no doorman and had more faith in astrology than in psychology. A spouse and children had not yet been in his stars, either.

Michael and I had both started our careers three years after our parents had divorced. Our complex family life had made us both feel the need for self-initiated pursuits. Michael got a guitar for Hanukkah when he was eight and hadn't put it down since. I had raised my hand to help out in the kindergarten the year I was eleven and had ever since been working with children. Ironically, the different paths we had taken as children led us both from Cleveland to New York City. I came to attend graduate school in a nationally known program, and Michael came a few years later to live his music in a place where a musician's life-style was welcome.

People who knew Michael and me well found a similarity in our sense of humor and in our use of language. We enjoyed these qualities in one another, as well as the comfort of being with someone whose story was so familiar. But the waitress could not have known this. What she had probably noticed was the bushy hair that was a family trait. But what she might not have recognized was the mark of two people who had developed identities in contrast to their parents—two people who were now old enough to be parents themselves, but were struggling for a way out of countercultures of their own designs.

■   ■   ■

Opal put Qimmy in the front of the shopping cart and glowered at the resulting burst of tears. Most children loved riding through the supermarket this way, but it cramped Qimmy's Tinkerbell style and made her feel too vulnerable to possible desertion. My reassurances fell on deaf ears. I knew that Franklyn had instructed Opal to do this on a prior shopping trip. Franklyn was trying to assess Opal's independent living skills and had not approved of Qimmy wandering about the store while Opal collected the food.

He had asked me to go to the store to follow up on the activity.

I walked beside Opal as she pushed the cart with her crying child down the narrow aisles. Queeny Martin had given her a list of things Qimmy liked to eat, and Opal was focused on obtaining these items, seeming to take in little else. I wondered if Mrs. Martin had included food that Opal liked to eat as well. Nothing seemed to tempt her; she shopped in a mechanical fashion.

Qimmy had stopped sobbing but still cried softly, and I felt at a loss to try to facilitate more positive interaction between the two of them. I concentrated on being generally friendly and helpful to Opal, supporting, I hoped, her maternal role. How Opal actually felt about having my company in the Red Apple was anyone's guess.

Suddenly we were cart-to-cart with a woman who obviously knew Opal.

"Hey, Opal," the woman exclaimed, "you're lookin' good."

Opal almost smiled and definitely nodded. Her friend, however, did not look good. She was painfully thin and glassy-eyed, and her shopping cart contained the sugary ingredients of a crack addict's snack. The only other item in the cart besides a sack of cane sugar and sugared cereal were Pampers for her baby, the listless inhabitant of a dirty snowsuit. Opal said something as they passed that I could not hear and proceeded with her shopping.

I wondered what Opal was thinking as we walked in silence. Her friend probably had custody of the neglected baby in the cart because the neglect had gone unreported, while Opal was escorted through the Red Apple because her homelessness had brought Qimmy to someone's attention. How did Opal feel when she saw addicted and neglectful mothers with more freedom than she had? I watched her walking down the aisle with the grocery cart and I had no clue. It was as if Opal lacked the freedom to experience her reactions but added their weight to the full shopping cart, which became harden to push with every step.

■ ■ ■

Ronnie had left her shadow people with me, but by now they had been erased from the board. As I took in Ronnie's presence that day I could feel the light boring through the shadows with an intensity that hurt. She sat unusually still for a moment, looking down until huge tears began falling onto her hands, which remained motionless in her lap.

"What?" I asked softly.

"My mother yelled at me," she choked, then swept the tears from her face with the back of her hand.

Hmmm. So far, this sounded like a normal parent-adolescent event, but maybe Ronnie was not used to normal adolescent events. "What happened?" I asked.

Ronnie took a deep breath. "I don't know, just . . ." More tears, now with audible crying.

"Take your time," I said.

"I just came in from my friend's house," she continued, "and I was making popcorn and hot chocolate in the microwave and . . ."

"And what?"

"She came in and started screaming." More crying, and now Ronnie's hands were twisting her red hair as if to demonstrate how tangled she was in the experience she was trying to describe.

"Screaming about what?" I inquired with some patience.

"I don't know. Something about locking the door with the chain."

"You forgot to lock the door?"

"No, but I just forgot to put the chain on . . . She didn't have to scream like that." Ronnie hiccuped.

"Are you angry?" I asked.

"No." Ronnie always denied anger with Sara.

"Sad?"

She nodded.

"Scared?"

"I'm scared," she repeated with relief, which seemed to surprise her. Safer to be scared than angry. "Yeah, I was scared, I guess. It was like out of the blue or something."

I nodded. "Does that happen a lot with you guys?"

Ronnie shook her head emphatically. "Never. My mom never yells at me."

"Except for today," I reminded her.

Ronnie shrugged. "Well, except today."

"What was different about today, then?"

She looked at me warily and reached for the marker board

and markers. "Nothing," she replied flatly. She began drawing vertical lines with each marker color, making a rainbow-like array but without the arch, placing one color beside the other. There was silence.

"Remember that thing you make when you're little?" she asked finally. She looked and sounded young. "You know, you take all different colors of crayons and you color really hard and you fill up the whole page, and then you take the black and color over the whole thing, and then you take your fingernail or a pencil or something and make scratches in the black, and the bright colors underneath show through and you make a design?"

I nodded.

"Well, therapy's like that for me sometimes, but it's the other way around. It's like the bright colors are on the top and then you make these little scratches and underneath it's all black." She shuddered, looking up at me for a response.

"All black and scary, like the shadow lady?" I asked her gently. "Sounds like it hurts." I looked for the hurt, intending to give comfort, but she had taken care of that herself. She was seated on the floor in front of the marker board, her knees to her chin, her arms crossed and holding her ankles, holding herself together for dear life.

■ ■ ■

"Where are the fathers?" asked Franny one morning.

I looked up from the easel paints I was preparing. I thought she wanted some information from the girls' charts regarding paternal history. I opened my mouth to reply, but she anticipated my answer.

"No, I mean, in *here*. They sometimes refer to Daddy in their play, but no one ever volunteers to play his part."

I considered this. "Well, we have the puppets and those rubber doll families." But come to think of it, the only kid who ever played with the puppets was Kendra, and she did this by sequestering herself in a corner behind a table to guarantee a lack of audience. Angie used the rubber doll family as transitional objects for her imaginary journeys to Puerto Rico. She packed them into an empty lunch box a couple of times each week and announced her departure to the airport.

"Maybe we do need something," I agreed. It made sense that they didn't use the daddy dress-up clothes we provided. It was an all-female group, and whoever ventured to be the father would probably be made fun of by the other girls, as well as be attacked because of oedipal anxieties. We smiled at each other to acknowledge that our own resistance had probably allowed us to be oblivious to the problem up till now. We were both very protective, both of our patients and of ourselves. We opened up the storage closet to see whether it held any toys that conveyed a male image. There were some Fisher-Price car garages; no, not exactly right.

"How about this?" Franny held up a deflated plastic blow-up toy with Mickey Mouse's painted image on the front. When inflated it stood taller than some of our children. Mickey was dressed in a top hat and a suit of sorts and sported giant black shoes.

"Yeah, I guess. That might do. It's definitely male and shouldn't be too threatening . . . I mean, a Disney character is a pretty benign figure." We pulled it out and took turns blowing into its hat, securing the rubber plug moments before the arrival of our crew. Mickey stood in a far corner of the room, ready for playmates.

The girls poured in looking weary. Angie was whimpering, 'Mitri was silent and sullen, and Kendra put her head down on the table. They looked as though they had been awake for many hours, although it was only 9 A.M.

"I don't know what's the matter with them today," announced Maimai as she hung up her hat and coat. Raquel unbuttoned her coat and gave a "who knows?" gesture in Maimai's direction. Then Maimai screamed, having caught sight of Mickey. "Come on, y'all." Angie and Kendra didn't budge, but 'Mitri and Raquel followed Maimai and all three lunged at the giant Mickey Mouse, punching him in unison over and over, again and again.

"Hey, what's going on? What's all the punching?" No one answered me, and instead they began adding a verbal dimension to their preemptive attack.

"There, that's good for you, you bastard. Don't you show your face around here again."

"Yeah, you motherfucker, I'll throw your ass in the street." Maimai tried to emphasize her point with a punch, but missed and hit 'Mitri's arm by mistake. 'Mitri wailed. "It was an accident. I'm sorry, it was an accident," Maimai chimed anxiously. Even 'Mitri understood this, and she stood crying without trying to take revenge. There was a momentary lull as Franny rubbed 'Mitri's arm and I reassured Maimai. Meanwhile Raquel looked eager to resume punching, glancing hopefully at 'Mitri for signs that the crying would abate. Kendra and Angie seemed thankful for the disruption. Kendra hated any show of violence. Angie, who did not know who her father was, longed for a male image to call her own and felt anxious at seeing this new possibility destroyed.

"What was happening before? Why was everyone punching Mickey?" I asked, returning to my original line of questioning.

" 'Cause he be botherin' us," 'Mitri explained grumpily.

"Well, he was new for you. I guess that his just *being* here bothered you," I ventured.

"Well, we beat him up *first* so he wouldn't bother us," Raquel explained with more patience than 'Mitri possessed.

"Damn," said Maimai. "Let's get out of here, anyway. I changed my lock so that bastard can't come in no more." She motioned her troops to come to the kitchen corner. "He not worth botherin' about anyway." They began rooting around in the cupboards to amass the usual collection of play foods and dishes. Kendra stayed at the table drinking her juice and began working on her drawing. Angie slowly approached Mickey Mouse. She stood looking at him. They were both somewhat pear-shaped and could stand eye-to-eye, only Mickey's top hat made him taller.

"What do you think?" I asked Angie, standing behind her and looking down into her face. "Should he stay?" Angie leaned back against me and nodded. She stood sucking one finger.

"My daddy doesn't like me," she said sadly.

"He doesn't? How do you know?" I asked her.

" 'Cause he don't come and visit me. He never came to my house."

"Do you know where your daddy lives, Angie?" Angie shook her head. "Maybe your daddy doesn't know where you live, either," I proposed. As far as I knew, no one, including Angie's grandmother, knew who her daddy was.

She considered this. "Could I write him a letter and tell him?" she suggested hopefully. Her hazel eyes were twinkling at me and her chubby hands were now petting my hair, making her imperfect logic difficult to refute.

"Let's write a letter and put down everything you'd like to say to your daddy if you could find him. We don't know where he lives yet, but if we ever find out you will have a letter to send him."

This satisfied Angie. "Get paper," she demanded. "I'll get a pencil from my book bag." We sat down to compose the letter. "Dear Daddy," she said, proud that she knew how to begin. She needed me to spell each word for her so that she could print. She then began fidgeting in her seat and chewing the eraser on her pencil. "I can't write no more," she whined after a moment.

"Okay, you tell me what to say and I'll write it down for you," I offered. She liked this.

"Dear Daddy, I am Angie. I am in the first grade." She pondered before continuing. "My mommy took drugs and died *porque* she wanted to. I don't want to stay with *abuelita porque* she don't need any more little girls." Angie's custodial grandparent had young daughters of her own. "Please come to my house at 2781 Fordham Road, Apartment 1B. Signed, Angie Ramos, six years." I helped Angie find an envelope, and she carefully folded the letter to fit it in. I opened my mouth to say something about her feelings of being so dispensable, but my words were interrupted by Kendra hiding her sobbing face in my shoulder, pointing blindly toward Mickey Mouse's corner. Raquel and Maimai were both straddling the toy, pulling him down and giggling, groaning with the sounds of adult sexual pleasure. I walked toward them with Kendra clinging to me. They did not interrupt themselves.

"Stop," I said. "You are really upsetting Kendra. You're doing what grown-ups do, and by playing that, it looks like it's okay for kids to have sex like grown-ups do, and Kendra knows that's not okay." They quieted down but did not get up. Finally Maimai let go and rolled off Mickey, and Raquel jumped to her feet and brushed her hands together.

"He not botherin' us anymore," Raquel said happily, and skipped back to the kitchen.

■   ■   ■

Betsy was eager to get down to business as usual. She was looking at a form that Franklyn had sent so that Preventive Services could keep track of Qimmy's progress. "Let's assess the situation as it is," she said, tapping her plastic cigarette against the doll plate that served now as a make-believe ashtray. "Opal is, for all intents and purposes, in residence with Queeny Martin, at least for the time being. She doesn't have to live in the subway. She supports herself on SSI in addition to contributions of clothing from Mrs. Martin. She is a volunteer at the Child Care Center and at times," Betsy said, smiling, "an asset to the infant room."

I nodded in agreement with all of this, crossing my legs, which were propped up on the bookkeeper's desk.

"Opal's daughter Qimmy will celebrate her fourth birthday next week, the day after Valentine's Day. She is a bona fide member of our preschool group, is well dressed and well cared for by Queeny Martin and sometimes by Opal, and is about the most agile kid I've got in the school, including kids two years older than she."

I smiled at this rosy report, anticipating what was to follow.

"On the other hand, Opal States only says about four words a day, even to Queeny, and less than that to Qimmy. You and Franklyn have taught her what to do with Qimmy in the supermarket, or what toys to buy for her, or how to feed her, and she does most of what you say. But I don't know. It's like she does it without being there, like she's on remote control with you guys pushing the buttons. The only time she acts like she feels anything is when she's holding a baby."

An accurate assessment, I concurred.

"Qimmy States comes to school every day. Her only words are to ask for food or to assert her possession over her dolls. She flits around the room clutching her baby, her watchful eyes staying fixed on the adults at all times, waiting for them to move in the direction of the graham cracker box, making sure that no one comes too close to her or gets too far away. Occasionally she gives up her guard duty to make subways with blocks and train cars."

I nodded again, still impressed with the quality of Betsy's therapeutic evaluation.

"But this isn't normal behavior!" Betsy exploded, losing all patience. "I want them to be . . ." She groped for a word which conveyed all her hopes for the Stateses.

"Normal?" I offered.

She hid behind her huge glasses for a moment, then nodded slowly.

"Yeah, I guess that's it. I just want them to forget about all the terrible things that have happened to them so they can benefit from what they have now."

"The problem is they can't benefit from what they have now unless they remember their feelings about all the terrible things that have happened in the past," I countered.

"But that doesn't make any sense," Betsy said, rolling her eyes at me.

"It's those missing feelings that keep Opal on remote control. But finding those feelings—"

She cut me off. "—is going to take a long time."

"It's true."

"Very reassuring. But it can't take *too* long, because if Qimmy is still wandering around school like Tinkerbell at age five, she's not going to make it in regular school. It kills me to think of putting her in special ed, because I have a feeling in spite of everything that she's smart."

"She is smart," I agreed, "but she's had to use her intelligence for survival. It may be a while before she feels safe enough to use it for other pursuits." The phone interrupted us and Betsy answered.

"Child Care Center." She held the phone away from her ear, taken aback by the food vendor's tirade, then hearing him out to be polite. She held up one finger to me as she listened, mouthing the words "one year" as I put on my coat to leave.

Her words followed me out of the door and onto upper Broadway. My path and my thoughts kept being disrupted by detours onto wooden construction-company walkways guiding pedestrians through the maze of renovations. None of these towers was being built to house Opal or others in her situation. They were apparently being built for "normal people" who could afford to purchase two-hundred-thousand-dollar cooperative apartments. It was getting very hard to be normal in New York City. Each time one of these co-op apartments was sold, Opal and Qimmy became less and less part of the norm.

That night when I went to sleep I became homeless, or maybe my apartment became home to so many things that it could no longer be home to me. Moss had grown everywhere and cobwebs had draped themselves across the windows and doorways. The furniture was shabby and neglected, and deep holes in the sofa's wooden frame had become nests to families of birds. Mice ate their way through rotten floorboards and searched in vain for sustenance. I was somehow looking in, but unable to get inside. "I can't live here anymore!" I shouted, awakening myself and startling my sleeping cat. I touched his ears for reassurance. "You wouldn't let mice come into our house," I whispered into his fur. He stared at me sympathetically for a moment, then blinked as if to dismiss the entire preposterous idea from his mind.

■ ■ ■

"I had a dream," began Ronnie, "and it wasn't about the shadow lady." She looked good today. Her face was no longer drawn from lack of sleep and her cheeks were bright from the effort of whatever activity she had been pursuing before our session. "I was little in the dream, and . . ."

"How little?" I interrupted her.

"Umm, well like, mm, I don't know, maybe like when we first moved to Manhattan. I was around six then. Anyway, it was in Central Park. Central Park is where I used to play. This time it was gigantic, bigger than the whole world, and it was all covered with snow, and there were no people except me." She thought for a second, hugging herself as though she were cold and pointing to her own chest to show me that she had been alone. "The sky was very cloudy. It was all one shade of gray and it covered the park like a dome, because except for some trees that was all I could see when I looked up. I mean, there were no buildings or anything."

"Hmm," I said.

"I was making snowballs, I was packing them really tight

until they were as dry as ice, and I started using them like bricks, and I built them in a circle all around me. I sat working in the middle of the circle, and I built them up higher and higher, like walls around myself. It was like there wasn't anyone else in the whole world. All I wanted to do was be inside, so I just kept working and working until the last snowball closed out the sky and the ceiling was finished, and I was inside the strongest, iciest igloo in the world, and then the dream was done."

"And you woke up?" I asked.

"Yep, that was it," she said, offering me an extended hand as though to show me it was empty of snow. Hmm, an igloo; cold but at the same time insulating.

"What kind of a dream was it?" I asked her. I looked for the answer in her eyes, but her face had become a mask of freckles and braces.

"What do you mean, what kind?" She was squinting at me, either because the sun was coming from the window behind me or because the question didn't make any sense to her.

"You know. Was it nice, scary, lonely, or what?"

She was quiet for a long time. "It was, I don't know, nothing. It was . . . too cold to feel, like the feelings were frozen or something."

"Why?" I asked quickly. She shrugged.

"Because they had to stay frozen," she retorted, anger in her voice. "*Because,* that's why. Because if they weren't frozen the snowballs would have melted and there wouldn't be an igloo anymore, and then . . ." She shivered.

"Then what?" I pursued. She shrugged and fell silent. I continued, "Then you'd be cold and all alone without a house like your shadow lady, like the homeless people on the subway?" She nodded, tears suddenly making a path down her cheeks.

"When I had this dream, I didn't think it was a bad dream. I thought it was nicer than the shadow lady dream, but now I don't know." She looked at me apprehensively.

"It looks like you think I might have done something that made the dream get scary."

"You *did* do something," she said accusingly.

"What?" I asked.

"I don't know. I don't know. Let's talk about it next time," she suggested, suddenly in a hurry. "I have to leave a few minutes early to go to a Spanish club meeting at school. It takes me a long time to get there because I have to go on the bus."

Hmm, also my fault that she's not healthy enough yet to ride the subway, I thought. Although I had the feeling that this would not be a problem very much longer.

"We'll talk about it next time," I agreed.

■ ■ ■

I couldn't wait to see Tina. I was bursting with children's metaphors: Kendra's nun fantasy; Maimai, Raquel, and 'Mitri's Mickey Mouse man; Ronnie's igloo. Opal and Qimmy had not yet achieved metaphor. They were prisoners of consciousness, denying themselves access to their unconscious for fear that the dreams would come to life and swallow them up. And then there were my own dreams, born of my association with Opal and Qimmy but awakening personal visions of long-neglected parts of myself.

Tina's husband, Mark, peered through the peephole of the front door, then unlocked and slowly opened it.

"Uh-oh," he said, looking stricken. "Come on in. You're going to kill me." I moved tentatively into the hallway. "Tina's sick. I was supposed to call you and tell you not to come today. Shit! I feel terrible." So did I. I just stood there staring at Mark, trying to take in that my train trip had been for naught. "Well, do you want to come in for a while? I could make some coffee. Tina's asleep and I've got the kids in the den." I peeked into the kitchen. The snowy yard was gleaming, and sunlight beat through the kitchen window and whitewashed the counter.

"I have an idea. I'll walk around the woods in back of your house and supervise myself, then I'll come in for tea."

Mark led the way to the back door. "Have a good time!" he called out after me. "That way, when Tina wakes up I can tell her that you had a good time and she won't kill me."

I waved Mark into the house and walked out into what might be the last snow of the northern county winter, thinking about Ronnie's igloo. She feared that having her own feelings would melt the igloo and leave her homeless like the woman in the subway who terrified her. She had to work hard to keep the igloo packed together, frozen into its chilly but gleaming and sheltering state. If the house-tree-person test that Betsy had mentioned earlier could be useful here, it implied that the igloo portrayed Ronnie's maternal image. It seemed that Ronnie had an unconscious assumption that behind Sara's strength and earth-mother image lay a terrible frailty. Perhaps Ronnie felt that Sara could not survive the heat of Ronnie's passion, that without Ronnie's constant efforts, the fragile ecosystem that Sara had designed for the two of them might collapse. In fact, a Ronnie who could go to school and was on the verge of being able to ride the subway was a Ronnie who might become more and more involved in her own adolescent drama, and less and less invested in the mother-child ecosystem. Maybe that's why Sara was screaming about unlocked doors. I sighed as I watched a parade of bubbles glide along the side of the streambed under a sheet of buckling ice. The truth as Ronnie felt it would unfold in her dreams, but getting the historical truth out of Sara seemed as likely as getting an autobiographical account from Opal States.

Meanwhile, this March I was feeling something I had never felt before, an impatience for spring. As a child of the Midwest I had always been content with cold and snow, but now I felt that something deep within me was defrosting and creating a parallel process between my patients and myself, all of us striving to move beyond the fortresses of our own design, struggling to remove NO TRESPASSING signs that we had posted on our own uncharted properties. I finished wandering the fenced-in territory of Mark and Tina's property and headed back to the house to have raspberry tea.

■   ■   ■

Sara sat in the butterfly chair, not wanting to be there. Not that she had ever really wanted to be there. She had always been more dutiful than eager in her work with me, but this evening there was an angry tone to her resistance.

"Ronnie is very forgetful lately," she explained.

Forgetting to hold up the walls of the igloo, I thought sleepily. It was a 9 P.M. session.

"What is she forgetting?" I questioned.

"I don't know," said Sara with impatience. "Locking the door, packing her lunch, things like that. Ronnie's always been very on top of things. Even when she was a little girl I could rely on her to remind me if I'd forgotten something." This made me think of something I'd seen on a poster on the bus recently. It was a picture of a black child captioned with a quote by Lucille Clifton that ran something like: "They want me to remember their memories but I keep on remembering mine." I repeated this to Sara. She smiled for the first time since arriving.

"Oh yeah, I remember seeing that and wanting to write it down." Then the smile disappeared. "I guess I like to think that Ronnie and I share most of our memories. I mean, that because we've always been together our minds work the same way. Lately, I don't know. I don't know what we share anymore." She had been talking loudly, but her voice suddenly became very soft, almost a whisper.

"Maybe sharing means something different at this age," I said, also softly. "Maybe it means each of you has her own experiences and memories but can talk about them with the other." Sara sat with that for a moment with her lips drawn in, her eyes looking at the floor.

"How long do you think it will take," she asked abruptly, "for Ronnie to finish here?" I had not anticipated this question. Neither did I know the answer. I didn't feel like going the usual route of turning the question back to her.

"That depends on Ronnie. I think the pace needs to be up to her. But tell me what you think about it being a longer process than you might have originally anticipated." Sara yawned, then seemed somewhat renewed.

"I left therapy as a last resort because I did anticipate it being a long, painful process, and I didn't think Ronnie needed that. But now it doesn't matter what I think," she said sadly, bitterly. "Ronnie thinks for herself."

■   ■   ■

The group had a case of spring fever. "Why we have to stay in this old room anyway?" Maimai complained, throwing herself down in the beanbag chair for emphasis. "Why can't we at least go out to the park or someplace?"

"There just be those crack dealers hanging around there," 'Mitri responded. "That where you wanna be?"

Raquel smiled teasingly. "Anyhow, you pee on yourself every time we go out somewhere." She directed this to Maimai.

"So?" said Maimai unperturbed. "I can't help it. It just come out."

"That's true?" Kendra asked Franny and me anxiously. "Her pee come out just like that?"

"That's how it feels to Maimai," Franny answered.

"Uh," Raquel responded. "She like a baby, then." They were sitting around the table, squeezing drops of assorted food colors into ice cube trays of water, creating designs to be frozen.

" 'Cept she never cry," observed 'Mitri. "Only stand there and suck her finger and don't say nothing."

"Why you don't cry?" Kendra asked Maimai softly. Maimai shrugged and said nothing but began to look concerned. She gave Kendra a look meant to ward off further questions.

"God cry," Raquel chimed. "My mommy told me that's where rain comes from."

"No," countered Angie. "Rain is *porque* my mommy's crying. She's in heaven and she cries when she misses me." Franny and I exchanged looks. On the one hand, the idea that Angie was worth missing was new. On the other hand, we worried about her fantasizing joining her mother in heaven in order to make her mother feel better. She was still setting fires and acting recklessly.

"How do you know, Angie?" I asked her.

"Because my *abuelita* told me." Franny and I both sighed inwardly. Getting Angie's grandmother to deemphasize the culturally familiar explanation of the lost parent's continuing life in heaven seemed hopeless, but it was a dangerous notion to a child with suicidal thoughts. If Angie's fantasies became more elaborate and her acting out did not abate, we might have to consider hospitalizing her for her own protection.

"Remember how we talked about how Mommy's soul is in heaven but her body's in the ground?" Franny reminded her.

"Her soul's missing me, then," Angie replied. That seemed reasonable.

"Unh-uh," Maimai retorted. "Rain is when my baby sister

cries. She in heaven, too, and she cry 'cause she's a baby and babies always be cryin'." I stared at Maimai, who was calmly pouring colored water from one container to another. She had never once directly acknowledged this lost child who so preoccupied her and whom she tried so desperately to bring back to life in her baby-nurturing play. "That's why I don't cry, 'cause I don't want to die, too," Maimai continued. There was silence. "I don't want to go to heaven without my mommy."

Finally 'Mitri spoke, disgusted with Maimai's naïveté. "You don't die from crying, you dumb-dumb. If you did, Kendra'd be dead by this time. She always crying." Maimai kept pouring the water over and over again. Kendra looked at me and Franny for guidance, but I was busy trying to grasp Maimai's formulation. Not only was Maimai fearful about letting herself get psychologically older than her sister's chronological age, she was afraid that allowing her feelings to live would paradoxically result in death. After all, the good, lively, laughing and crying toddler from the photograph book had engendered enough rage to be killed and now lay crying into the clouds. Maimai preferred her own puddles, which brought predictable punishments. I put my arm around Maimai, who was sitting next to me, and through teary eyes watched the drops of color splash into her water design.

"Maybe Maimai will feel safe enough to cry some day while she's with us," Franny answered 'Mitri, "and then she'll find out that crying is safe." Maimai looked relieved that the matter had come to some closure, shook her wet fingers into the air, spraying us with her unshed tears, and dried her hands on a paper towel.

■ ■ ■

For a moment, it was springtime and birds were singing. I opened my eyes and they were still singing; the April morning music accompanied my clock radio's blinking proclamation that it was 5:04 A.M.

Birds sing in New York and no one knows it, I thought, and returned to sleep.

My apartment was cluttered with furniture. It was my furniture, but everything had been taken out of place and left to stand about the room looking awkward and helpless, as though each item felt embarrassed that it could not perform its usual function.

I wandered through the house in disbelief, angry. Who could have done this to my things? I examined everything to make sure all remained intact and nothing was missing. Finally satisfied that everything could be accounted for, I breathed a sigh of relief and stood still for a minute.

The sweet smell of flowers emanated from a corner of the room I could not see. I peered around a mountain of furniture to follow the smell. . . . A jungle garden had grown from the kitty litter box. Shiny green stems sprouting thick leaves filled with invisible milk surrounded giant orange-and-yellow petals, which encased long, pollen-covered stamens. Bees fed on the flowers, and butterflies rested there. I came closer, tiptoeing in case I might scare the butterflies away. But they were not afraid. As I stared into the garden, I found new forms of life on every leaf of every plant. There were spiderwebs full of shimmering dewdrops, whose brilliantly colored resident spiders were both intriguing and terrifying. There were ladybugs whose shells were covered with intricate designs, and shiny black ants that were larger than life.

A voice began to overwhelm the scene. It was louder than the ladybug's design; louder than the city birds or the drone of the sanitation truck. It was telling me the time. Time to wake up. Time for work.

A cat's tongue tickled my ear. I opened my eyes. There was no evidence of the garden, except for the lingering smell of spring.

■   ■   ■

Qimmy was lying in Queeny Martin's lap, whimpering as Queeny carefully parted, combed, and braided tiny cornrows into her hair. "This child's tender-headed," Queeny said, frustrated by Qimmy's cries.

"Like I was," Opal added from across the room. We both looked at her. She rarely said anything spontaneous like this. "My mama used to do my hair that way. Aunt Kelly said I always be fussing." There was a hint of a smile.

"Do you remember?" I asked quickly. Never mind what Aunt Kelly said. Opal shook her head. It didn't matter. I was jubilant. She had mentioned her mother for the first time and had expressed an identification with Qimmy. "You should probably comb Qimmy, then, 'cause maybe you'd remember what it felt like. You'd be nice and gentle," I suggested. Queeny looked up, immediately seeing the opportunity here.

"You want Mommy to make you look real pretty?" she asked Qimmy, gathering her up to transfer her to Opal's lap. Qimmy seemed willing to give it a try. She buried herself in an afghan Queeny had pulled off the back of the sofa and put on Opal's lap. Opal pursed her lips and studied the back of Qimmy's head. Queeny wisely got up and offered me some tea, interrupting my breathless study of the mother and child finally receiving one another. I got up and followed Queeny to the kitchen area, where I was handed a cup of tea and a copy of some legal papers explaining the status of the impending adoption. I skimmed the page of legalese, gleaning only that everything seemed in order and that it was a matter of waiting the requisite time. Opal and Queeny had gone to court twice already.

"Not too sure what this means," Queeny mused, "but my friend Mr. Trevor says everything's coming along nicely." Neither one of us had any idea whether Housing would approve Opal's residence in the project even when the adoption was official. Yet it was clear that the adoption process had helped Opal already. She felt cared for and in some way restored. The proof was in the living room, where a mother sat gently braiding her daughter's hair.

■ ■ ■

"Let's see, where should I start?" began Ronnie. Her red hair no longer hung down to touch her hands but lay curling on her shoulders. Her teeth looked different as well, as though there were more or less braces than before, but I could not tell which. "I rode the subway all week long," she announced, beaming.

I beamed back. "How was it?"

"Well," she said with hands clasped in front of her. "Promise you won't tell anyone." I said nothing, as I thought I had promised that from the start. "I pretended I was in the story of "Three Billy Goats Gruff," She giggled. "You know the part where the goats keep trying to go over the bridge but there's a troll who lives underneath and won't let them pass?" I nodded. "I pretended the homeless people were the trolls and they'd let me pass if I paid the toll. So I put a lot of change in my pocket every morning, and every time I saw a homeless person I'd give them some, and then I ran past until I got where I was going. Or else, if I was already on the train, I'd pretend that giving them money would make them let me off when I needed to get off." I considered this for a while.

"So you bought your passage to safety," I commented. She agreed, nodding vigorously.

"And that way their eyes didn't scare me. Sometimes, after I gave money they looked at me with, you know, nice eyes." Her own nice eyes seemed occupied with the side window view of the street, perhaps avoiding mine. She was silent for a moment. "It seems weird to pay you," she said abruptly. I waited. "I mean, Sara always gives me a check for you at the end of the week. I don't know . . . I wish she would just pay you herself."

"How come?" I inquired. "Does it make me something like the troll?"

She smiled. "It's like Sara's making you a troll."

"And what would happen if I didn't get my money?" I asked, hoping she could elaborate on the metaphor.

"You'd keep me," she said gleefully.

"Hmm. So you think Sara pays me to give you back to her?" Ronnie nodded. This was an accurate perception. "So what about the homeless women? If you didn't pay them, would they keep you too?"

Ronnie shivered. "They'd capture me in their eyes like in the dreams."

That's right, I remembered, she was afraid of seeing her own reflection in their eyes.

Then she asked, "You know what my grandma says?" I didn't, but was interested. "She says when I was little I used to cover my eyes when I got scared."

"What used to make you scared?" I asked. Ronnie shrugged. "Don't ask me. You have to ask my grandma."

That suddenly seemed like a great idea, bringing the grandmother in. How resistant would Sara be to that?

"Okay," I agreed. "Tell your grandma I'd like her to come

in one of these days." Ronnie smiled as though the idea of her grandmother sitting in one of the butterfly chairs was an incongruous image. Then she was quiet for a moment.

"I know something that Sara doesn't know I know," she said in a secretive tone. I waited. "My dad pays child support for me."

"Why is that a secret?" I asked.

"I don't know, but I know Sara doesn't want to tell me. I figured it out a long time ago." Ronnie's arms were folded across her chest; in that pose she looked very adult. It was a paradox, I thought, that she should look adult in the moment when she acknowledged being somebody's child.

"How does it feel to know that?" I asked her.

"God!" she exploded, instantly turning into a teenager. "Why do you always ask me that? You sound like a broken record!"

"You sound like you don't want to tell me," I responded. She suddenly reached for her jacket and held it to her chest like a baby doll.

"Do you think he sends money because he wants to or because the court makes him?" she asked with effort.

"I don't know. What do you think?"

Ronnie shrugged.

"I guess Sara would know the answer to that," I said.

"Yeah," Ronnie agreed, putting her coat on to leave. "But if I ask her, she'll go to bed and pull the covers over her head and never come out." Then she gave me the check that she did not want to give me, in order that she might return home, and left me with the image of Sara hidden under the covers.

■ ■ ■

This spring, Qimmy had a new occupation other than baby doll–tending. This became evident as I approached the three-year-old area of the Child Care Center, ducking a clothesline of dripping paintings, all with Qimmy's name in the upper right-hand corner in Maria's printing. Qimmy was working on painting number seven when I arrived, which was very similar in design to paintings number one, two, three, four, five, and six. Qimmy stood with her eyes glued to the easel, applying several coats of red paint to a large spot on the lower left-hand part of the paper. Then she took black and painted over the middle of the red, creating two small black circles, the circular patterns superimposed to make indentations in the many coats of wet red paint.

"Qimmy's making flies," Monica said proudly from her place at the water table. She had a bird's-eye view of Qimmy's productions.

"Yeah, and she talked yesterday. She said 'Mommy,' " Gilbert added. These two were apparently in charge of monitoring Qimmy's progress when I was not present.

"That's great," I responded with enthusiasm. I moved closer to the clothesline to get a good look at painting number one. If it was a fly, it was a fly that had been squished against a wall. "What's this red part under the fly?" I asked Monica, curious about her association.

"Apples," Monica said cheerfully.

Maria smiled at me from the block area, where several children were assembling an elaborate set of train tracks. "Qimmy," she called out, "tell Lesley who made your hair so beautiful." Qimmy took her paintbrush off the paper and looked up at me as if I had just walked in.

"Mommy," she said with a smile.

"And who bought your shoes?" Maria continued.

"Mommy buy my shoes," Qimmy repeated.

" 'Mommy buy' is the phrase of the week," said Maria giggling. "To hear Qimmy tell it, Mommy has bought everything we have in our room." This was interesting. Qimmy was attributing some of the magic that toddlers endow their mothers with to Opal. She seemed to have been unable to do this before, probably because Opal had been helpless to provide for her for so long. Before Queeny Martin, Qimmy had been provided for by a succession of strangers, whose faces were sometimes attached to hands bearing juice or milk or hot dogs. Qimmy had learned to look to the outside world for what she needed and to take without making connections. Although Queeny Martin had kept Qimmy for almost a year before Opal came to the day-care center, Qimmy rarely gave back to Queeny the way most children do to the adults who care for them, with spontaneous hugs, smiles, or songs sung in the adult's honor. This tribute to Mommy was something new, and in spite of the somewhat ominous mood created by the squished-fly paintings hanging overhead, I felt hopeful about Qimmy.

"Has Opal heard Qimmy say that?" I queried Maria. I didn't know whether Opal was here today or not, as the baby group had gone for a stroller walk. Maria's smile faded.

"Opal doesn't understand," she whispered. "She thinks Qimmy is lying. She said Franklyn bought Qimmy shoes for her." Hmm. This was a more complicated task: getting Opal to believe in herself as all-powerful Mommy, helping her understand that the patterns she braids into Qimmy's hair are changing not only Qimmy's self-image but her own.

■ ■ ■

I sat staring at Ronnie's grandmother Rena; I was in a butterfly chair, Rena in a straight chair. "If I sit down on that I'll never get up," Rena had protested with humor. I had smiled and indicated another place for her to sit, grateful that her comment required no verbal response because her presence left me speechless. She was petite, about Ronnie's height, and her red hair gone gray had been colored by an orange dye which would have made her easy to spot in a crowd. Her aqua skirt was short and tight, and the matching jacket, worn open, revealed a black designer blouse, sheer and low-cut in the front. Under the blush, eye shadow, and penciled eyebrow lines I thought I could see Ronnie's pleasant features. What was striking was the absence of any reflection of Sara. Rena's dramatic image made Sara pale by comparison—or perhaps Sara looked at Rena and felt the need to remain incognito. Something about Rena's face was scary; it resembled an ancient carving deep with the scars of time beyond reach, but it had been face-lifted into a smooth and shining countenance by a plastic surgeon, attempting to restore Rena's beauty without understanding her pain. Thus she appeared as an incongruous blend of age and adolescence. In spite of efforts to coordinate color and fabric, she did not seem to fit together.

"So this is it," she said, looking around the room. "This is where Ronnie comes to tell her little secrets. Everyone should have such a place, no? A place to tell someone who might understand."

"What do you think would help me to understand Ronnie?"
I asked. Rena shrugged.

"Ronnie is precious the way she is, you know? I wouldn't
want she should change a hair on her head. So she doesn't like
to ride on the subway. Who does? In a couple of months I am
planning to cash in some saving bonds that my late husband took
out in Ronnie's name. After that she can ride in a taxi every day
if she likes."

This was interesting. Ronnie's symptom had Rena's blessing,
if not Sara's.

"So Ronnie's subway fears don't worry you?"

Rena dismissed them with a wave of her hand. "A child,
particularly a young teenager, goes through things."

I thought about this a minute. "Did Sara go through things
like this as a teenager?" Rena's face clouded. She rubbed her
neck, which then lost its powdery sheen and emerged wrinkled.

"Sara was not a very strong girl; she was not like my Ronnie.
Of course, I didn't know that then. How does a mother know what
is going on in the mind of her child? She is smart, she does well
in school, I think that means something positive."

I nodded, encouraging her to continue.

"But Ronnie has friends, and this Sara never had. And
Ronnie plays the games that children play. She joins the cheer-
leaders and the newspaper. She does not let life pass her by.
Sara was not a doer as a child. She was serious and studious, but
she was not a doer like Ronnie, and when the kids started to be
concerned with their clothes, and boyfriends, and parties, Sara
was only getting bored. She was all the time in the house. Her
father and I could never get her to go out until she left for the
Peace Corps. She was home all the time and bored all the time.
Then, all of a sudden, she announces that she will join the
Peace Corps and she becomes a doer, and for her this is the
happiest time of her life."

"Hmm," I said, thinking out loud. "First she didn't want to
leave the house at all, then when she did she went thousands of
miles away."

Rena fumbled in her purse for some chewing gum.

"That's exactly what I said to my husband," she said, seemingly unconscious that the gum was garbling her speech as she folded it into her mouth.

"So in the end Sara's strength surprised you," I said, thinking I understood. Rena shook her head. It was as though the shaking were a ritual that magically undid the face-lift and gave me a glimpse of the fifty-year-old carving.

"In the end she was not strong," Rena said, fingering her brightly polished nails the way Ronnie often did, "because she had to come back, and even though Sara came back with a beautiful baby, again she got bored, but this time the boredom turned to despair." She looked around the room before continuing. "She wanted to kill herself," she whispered. I felt a shiver as the source of Ronnie's dream imagery became a cold reality. An igloo was a perfect metaphor for a desperate and suicidal mother, frozen by depression, clinging to her child for warmth in a house that had no windows to the outside world. The muted slam of my front door startled me and I jumped.

"I'm sorry," I said to Rena. "I'm not expecting anyone."

"It's Ronnie!" Rena exclaimed. "I told her to come and meet me here since I was in Manhattan. I didn't think it would take me long. I didn't think I had so much to say that would help my granddaughter." At that moment, Ronnie burst in.

"Are you done?" she asked Rena breathlessly. Then, "Hi," she said to me shyly.

"Since you're here, I'm done," Rena answered her, holding out her hand for Ronnie to take. They were warm in each other's presence.

"Did you ask her why I used to cover my eyes when I was little?" She directed this to me.

"Not yet, sweetheart," Rena answered for me. "But I will come back and we'll remember to talk about it another day." Ronnie nodded approvingly. "I have homework now," Rena said, laughing. "My homework is to remember what a beautiful baby you were." She fingered the ends of Ronnie's hair. Ronnie seemed unperturbed.

"Okay, Grandma. I only have an hour. I have a newspaper meeting after that." Ronnie waved at me and moved toward the door.

"I'll call for another appointment," Rena promised. "And to be with this one I need an appointment, also. She only has an hour at fourteen years old. What will I do in a couple of years? Maybe leave a message on her answering machine?"

Ronnie rolled her eyes. "Come on, Grandma." They left hand in hand.

■　■　■

Maimai and Angie entered the room holding hands, exchanging knowing looks. Franny and I exchanged looks of our own. This was certainly an unusual and perhaps unholy alliance. 'Mitri, Raquel, and Kendra spilled in after Maimai and Angie, seemingly delighted that the group was intact once again after a siege of chicken pox had diminished the ranks for some days.

"Look," Raquel said joyfully, producing Kendra's left arm. "Her chicken pops don't be contagious no more. My mama checked her before we came." Raquel took great pride in her mother's standing in the community as someone with health-care experience. Kendra broke away from Raquel's grip and ran to me for a hug. 'Mitri peeled off the sweater her mother had bundled her into. 'Mitri had had a very bad case. Franny hung the sweater carefully over the back of a chair. It was white and looked as if it might have previously been worn only to church or for special occasions.

"Let me know if you get cold, 'Mitri," Franny reminded her. 'Mitri rolled her eyes. It was a warm May day, but the sweater was one of the few protective measures we had seen 'Mitri's mother able to take on 'Mitri's behalf.

"I think Mommy was worried because you were so sick," I offered.

'Mitri looked blank. "I'm not sick now," she said in an off-hand way. It seemed impossible for 'Mitri to relinquish her role as a "parent." Connection to her own feelings of vulnerability was rare and usually triggered an explosion of rage at the nearest perceived enemy rather than at the addicted parent who was the source of her pain.

A crashing noise came from the other side of the room. Maimai and Angie were methodically tossing a set of large wooden blocks from the slatted wooden crate that housed them.

"Hey!" yelled 'Mitri in an accusing tone.

"Shut up," said Maimai sternly.

'Mitri shut up. She did not like to offend Maimai, whose friendship she courted loyally. She shrugged and went over to the easel to paint, occasionally peering over the top to keep track of Maimai and Angie's activity.

"Can we play?" Raquel had decided that it was better to join those two than to leave them to their own devices. She had Kendra by the arm again. Maimai considered this.

"Well, you two can help Angie then," she agreed. She was loading Angie's pudgy arms with blocks. Angie in turn dumped the blocks into a big pile in the corner. Raquel and Kendra formed a line behind Angie, eager for their allotment of blocks.

Maimai's smile grew; she looked like a pharaoh who had had the good fortune to acquire new slaves.

"But what are we making?" demanded Raquel.

"You'll see," Maimai retorted. She smirked gleefully at Angie, who was so delighted to be favored in this way that she skipped in a circle.

"Stop!" Maimai said abruptly, after the last blocks had been added to the pile. "Come on, Angie," she summoned, "push these over here."

She and Angie rolled the wooden crates away from the window.

"But what about us?" Kendra and Raquel clamored.

"Oh, y'all can't play this part," Maimai said, dismissing them with a wave.

"Franny!" screamed Raquel, on the verge of tears.

"You know, Maimai, Kendra and Raquel asked if they could play and you said yes, and then you let them work very hard for you."

"Oh, all right" Maimai said, exasperated. "Come on, you all. Let me tell you in your ear."

They huddled together to share the secret. 'Mitri remained at the easel, eyeing the group anxiously.

"You can ask to play, too," I told 'Mitri, but she shook her head. She continued to work on her painting: a blend of deep colors rising from the bottom of the page like an ancient monster rising from the sea.

I was studying 'Mitri's creation when I heard the jarring cries of distressed babies coming from the other side of the room. Franny, 'Mitri, and I looked up to see that the crates had been transformed into giant cribs and the five- and six-year-olds had regressed into infants screaming their neediness.

'Mitri dropped her paintbrush.

"They're babies," she said quietly, looking ashen.

"Yes, they're babies for now," I said. "Later they'll grow up to be big like always. They're pretend babies."

'Mitri covered her ears with her hands and shut her eyes tightly.

"Let's go see what these babies want," Franny suggested. "Maybe if we take care of them they won't need to cry."

This idea reassured 'Mitri. She could respond as a parent to defend against the pull of this mass regression.

"What you want?" she demanded sharply, approaching the cribs.

The three of us looked down at the babies. Maimai's hands were fists, her feet were kicking, and her body was small and tight. Her wide-open mouth and squinting eyes filled her reddening face with feeling that charged the desperate cries. Angie was her soft and floppy cribmate, lying beside her whimpering into her pillow, fingering Maimai's long cornrows, which touched Angie's pillowcase. Raquel and Kendra were in the next crib, alternating between crying and giggling.

"Maybe they would like their bottles," Franny suggested to 'Mitri over the din. 'Mitri ran for the bottles and handed one to each crying baby.

Raquel and Kendra stopped immediately and sucked contentedly on their leftover juice, suddenly more serious in their baby roles. Angie took the bottle from Franny and continued to whimper softly as she drank. Maimai continued to cry and would not open her eyes to see the bottle, nor would she open her fists to grab it. I reached into the crib and lifted Maimai into my lap.

She arched and stiffened, then melted as the bottle found its way into her mouth.

For several moments there was only the sound of sucking, interrupted by an occasional whimper from Angie. 'Mitri was kneeling beside Kendra and Raquel's crib, waiting anxiously for the bottles to empty and anticipating the collective return to older childhood that I had predicted.

"Remember when we were talking about Maimai being afraid to cry?" I asked. 'Mitri looked up and the babies continued to suck. "Today she figured out that being a baby and crying is safe. She used to be afraid that crying would mean that she would have to go far away, too far away from us and her mommy. But look, she's crying and she is still here."

Angie pulled the bottle out of her mouth and sat up abruptly.

"Unh-uh!" she countered, "Maimai and I did went away and we died. Then we got borned again. That's how we got to be babies," she said brightly.

I looked down at Maimai for confirmation, but she was too busy being a baby to respond.

"What do you mean, Angie?" Franny asked.

"*Mi abuelita* says when you die you get borned again, so me and Maimai played that we got borned again, and see . . ." She pointed at Maimai, who indeed acted newly born.

"But you and Maimai didn't die," Kendra said solemnly, nervously.

"So," Angie shrugged, "we could have died if we wanted to, but we just didn't want to."

"You didn't want to and you didn't have to because, look, you and Maimai and Kendra and Raquel were babies without having to die first. You can stay yourselves but remember how it felt to be little."

"Get up, Maimai." 'Mitri interrupted my interpretation. She still needed to see that this regression was not permanent. Her voice was robotic and her face looked paralyzed with worry.

I sat Maimai up and her bottle fell from her hand as she opened her eyes.

"Shut up, 'Mitri," she said, "else Freddy Kruger gonna put firecrackers in your mouth."

'Mitri breathed a sigh of relief. The woman-child upon whom she depended to spin threats as terrifying as her own inner fantasies was back on the job.

■   ■   ■

Queeny Martin fainted while standing in the checkout line at the Red Apple. She was rushed to St. Luke's Hospital and admitted for a blood-pressure crisis. She was allowed to have visitors. Opal States had been informed.

I listened to Franklyn's voice giving me this news three times over, rewinding my answering machine after assimilating the message, hoping Franklyn's tone would give me some clues about the severity of Mrs. Martin's condition. But Franklyn's voice was as steady as the anchorman's on the six o'clock news, his emotional ties to the Martins and Stateses masked by formality. I tried not to panic. Queeny was sick, not dead. I called Betsy.

"Not only is Opal visiting Queeny every day," Betsy said "but she is refusing to leave her. Queeny has phoned to ask that Qimmy be sent home with Andre, who lives in the same project. That's what has been happening for the last two nights. Qimmy is a wreck and she is not being her passive Tinkerbell self about it, either. She's mad as hell. She's knocking down the other kids' block towers, pulling hair, grabbing toys. She finally got that swat on the behind that Maria has been promising her all year for deliberately pouring a quart of milk all over the floor." Betsy stopped to inhale; plastic cigarettes had been replaced by real ones again.

"That's amazing!" I was ecstatic. "Qimmy's not taking this lying down; she's protesting the separation! That means she's attached." Qimmy was acting like the toddler who tried to recover the lost object, rather than sinking into despair or taking refuge in the detached state that was so familiar to her.

"Wonderful," Betsy replied sarcastically. "I'll be sure to tell that to Maria."

"Tell Maria to read to her about the hospital, so that she gets a mental picture of where Queeny and Opal are. I'll see what I can do about getting Opal to come home occasionally."

"You better hope Queeny can come home permanently," Betsy said. "I don't know if they are ready to go solo."

I didn't know either, but I reassured Betsy. I believed that Queeny had made an agreement with God: she would take her place in heaven only when Opal and Qimmy were strong enough and not before.

The hospital was a microcosm of the streets where Queeny and Opal lived, with one exception: here legal drugs replaced illegal ones. The patients breathed easier from behind their oxygen masks or as they wheeled themselves through the shabby halls, greeting their neighbors, offering concern and encouragement. It was as if trading gold jewelry and leather name-brand sneakers for bathrobes and hospital-issued slippers helped to recreate the healthier community spirit that had characterized this neighborhood before the invasion of crack. If people here were afraid for their lives, at least the threat did not come from among themselves.

"You're lookin' real fine," an elderly roommate was telling Queeny as I entered the room.

To me Queeny looked peaked. The large hospital bed dwarfed her, and I felt disarmed at seeing her now fragile frame minus the bulky cooper-buttoned navy-blue sweater that was always part of her uniform. I stood in the doorway trying to collect myself before she noticed me, but it was too late.

"Now you came all the way up here to see me and you're just gonna stand in the doorway," she scolded.

I smiled and stepped closer. "How do you feel?" I asked her.

"Better every day," she promised, the patient reassuring the social worker. "Not myself I'm worried about."

She gestured with her eyes to the far corner of the room, where Opal sat asleep in an armchair.

"I can't get my daughter," she said, emphasizing this phrase for the benefit of the nurse's aide tending a patient next to her, "to leave."

I stared at Opal, amazed at what I was seeing—Opal asleep under a roof not her own.

"She's exhausted," Queeny said, as if reading my mind. "Been here without a break. I'm worried for Qimmy. Probably thinks we deserted her."

I nodded, still amazed that Opal could rest. "And Qimmy's angry about it, too," I added.

Queeny looked concerned.

"It's a good kind of angry," I said quickly. "It shows she knows who belongs to her."

"All right then," Queeny said with a sigh, "but what about Opal? She needs to see to Qimmy, but she won't budge. Just sits and watches me, then sleeps. Yesterday I had her reading to me from the Bible. Not much of a talker, but a good reader," she mused.

"She probably got scared she'd lose you," I answered, also scared.

"Dr. Stein said I'll make it home," Queeny said slowly, "but the good Lord won't leave me down here forever." She looked at me with faded but pleading eyes; suddenly she seemed worn with worry.

"I know," I answered, confirming her unspoken concern. "I'll do what I can." Small comfort, since I had no idea what that might be.

"All right then." Queeny seemed relieved despite my doubts and closed her eyes, "just for a minute." She leaned back into her pillow, but her eyes remained closed as sleep pulled her toward the respite from responsibility that would allow her to heal.

I felt weak at the prospect of inheriting the responsibility that Queeny needed to relinquish. I wanted to wake Opal and usher her out, send her home to Qimmy and send myself home to learn how to live my own life instead of other people's. I twisted my hair into a knot and smoothed my wrinkled skirt.

"Opal," I whispered, walking toward her.

Her eyes opened instantly and she appeared fully alert.

"Queeny's asleep. Let's go. Qimmy needs to see you."

"Qimmy's with Andre in 3-D," Opal responded with a hollow voice.

"I know, but she needs *you*. She needs to know that you didn't disappear and that you are all right. She needs you to explain about Queeny."

Opal sat still, her dark brow furrowed, her lips pursed to fight emotion.

"Queeny's okay, Opal. Dr. Stein told her she'll be able to go home in a few days. We both know that Queeny is an old lady—" I struggled for the words, but Opal cut me off.

"Queeny's sick 'cause of me," she blurted.

" 'Cause of you?" I questioned in an incredulous tone. But for Opal, there was no question about it. Guilt spilled from her eyes in giant tears that fell between her parted knees onto the cold floor.

"What?" I asked softly, pulling up a chair beside her. But this was not easy to answer, because Opal, who perhaps had not cried for many years, was not used to talking through her tears. Many sobbing and choking sounds came before there were words. Finally she said, "She don't see well. Didn't know the date on the pressure pills was . . ." She could not continue, but she could cry, a high-pitched suffering cry that came from deep within the caverns of her well-guarded emotional life, a cry that made her usual speaking voice sound like an echo of her real self.

As I sat listening to those cries, providing tissues stolen from another patient's dressing table, shutting out all sounds of pain and healing save Opal's, it occurred to me that in this catharsis was a message that Opal's paralysis was perhaps partially due to guilt, the kind of guilt felt by the omnipotent toddler whose belief might have been, "My mommy's dead because of me, because I couldn't save her, because she sometimes made me angry, because I wanted Daddy's strong holding, too." If anger kills, it must be prevented at all costs. And in order to protect yourself, you had also better stay away from other people's angry hands— whether they are raging, choking hands, or the resentful hands that hold the key to your hotel room.

But why did Opal choose to bear the burden of survival without the company of feelings? Clearly, my assessment of Opal as having no access to emotion was incomplete. Guilt clung to her like thick green moss clings to a forest floor. And she clung to her guilty feelings for dear life. She held on to this blanket of guilt, without which she truly would have frozen. She clung to it as a toddler carries a security blanket to remind herself of Mother. Indeed, guilt was her lifeline, evidence that her feeling self still lived. It was necessary to proceed cautiously. Too much relief might leave her feeling free of this maternal connection, an orphan with no past.

"Now it will be different," I said softly, "because now we know that Queeny needs help to read the prescriptions, so you and I will be able to help her. Before, none of us knew, so we couldn't do anything to help."

Opal hid her face in her hands and let the sobs slowly subside. She didn't speak, but she was very vulnerable, the tears having melted the usual resistance.

"We gotta go find Qimmy," I continued. "I bet she thinks all of this is her fault."

Opal peered at me incredulously from behind her parted hands.

"Qimmy can't even read. She only four." Opal looked as me as though I'd taken leave of my senses.

"You and I know that," I said, gathering my things, "but kids always think they are the cause of everything."

Opal smiled with her eyes, pursed her lips, pulled her coat off the back of her chair, and headed toward the door.

■   ■   ■

I sat cross-legged on a butterfly chair in my office waiting for Ronnie.

"Don't let this case take you out of your office," Jacob had said. I felt relieved recalling his words. I did not want to leave my office. The midsummer air was hot and heavy with the tension of the crowded streets. Buildings seemed to be melting in the July sun. Old people stood fanning themselves in the withering heat. Babies cried. Passersby seemed guarded and resentful of one another, as if every pedestrian suspected the others of having personally gulped the last pocket of breathable air. Teenagers who had nowhere to turn became angered by the lack of breathing space and began to rove in restless groups, attacking randomly, seeking release from feelings of entitlement.

I did not want to leave my office, but I knew it went beyond the illusion of safety provided by the walls. I was experiencing a shift, a need to attend to the neglected inner space decorated by cobwebs in my dreams and inhabited by every form of life save my own unborn children. I was beginning to fear that they would never be born unless I spent more time in those spaces—time that went beyond the analytic hour. It was difficult to attend to those spaces while running around the city practicing "we deliver" psychotherapy.

"Hi!" Ronnie said bouncily, startling me. "The door was open." I had left it open for her.

Her face was sunburned pink, although the weather had been cloudy. Her fair skin must burn easily. But she did not seem oppressed by the heat; in fact, she seemed buoyant, riding a wave of optimism.

"Hi," I answered.

She sat down on the chair opposite me, then shrugged and giggled. "I don't know what to say today." It looked more like "I don't know who you are today." She was regarding me with blank eyes.

I waited. She said nothing.

"For a while now, I've been a troll," I reminded her, "along with the homeless women in the subway."

"Oh, oh yeah," she recalled with an exaggerated head-tapping gesture. Her earrings clanked. "I forgot." She was still all smiles, even with remembering. But suddenly the smile faded and she sat squinting as if trying to gain an inward focus.

"I had a dream about that," she said slowly, "only I think it was Sara who was the troll." She covered her eyes as if it were impossible to look at Sara and me simultaneously.

"I was in a dark place walking somewhere, kind of in a hurry. Then I happened to look down and the floor was clear, like ice maybe. And when I looked through it I could see a troll with Sara's face. I tried to keep walking because I was going somewhere, but the troll didn't want me to go any farther, so she started reaching her hand right through the floor. It was like a giant soap bubble or something. She tried to grab me and pull me through. I moved back to a solid part of the floor so she couldn't reach me." Ronnie looked at my floor for a minute and then back at me.

"She started getting really mad—the troll, I mean—since she couldn't reach me, and she started getting all red and her hair was really wild and she started puffing up in a weird way. I put my hands over my ears because I thought she might explode, like a balloon. But she didn't explode," Ronnie amended, her voice softening. "She started looking"—Ronnie looked down, one hand shading her eyes from the scary vision—"like . . . dead or something. Like blank and scary."

"You're putting your hands over your eyes," I commented.

"Huh?" She looked up, bewildered.

"When you talk about the scary Sara-troll looking dead, you put your hands over your eyes. I remember you wanted me to ask Rena why you used to cover your eyes when you were little. Maybe it was something about Sara that scared you?"

"Huh?" she said again, squinting at me. "No. It was just in the dream. In real life Sara's just . . . you know." She rolled her eyes either in exasperation with me or to acknowledge Sara.

"What? What is Sara? Just what?"

"Impossible to change," Ronnie blurted.

I nodded for her to continue.

"I mean, Sara just wants to keep going. She never wants to stop, even for weekends. Sara would be happiest if every day were Monday."

"And what would happen to Sara if every day were Sunday?" I asked.

"She would just stop, I guess, shrivel up like . . . God!" she exploded, suddenly furious with me. "Why do you ask me things like that?"

"You asked me why you used to cover your eyes when you were little. I think the dream was telling you something about that."

"I asked you to ask Rena, which you didn't do," she corrected me bitterly.

I looked at her face. Her eyes were narrow, with a rage I had never seen before. The braces on her clenched teeth looked like barbed-wire fences beyond which the enemy could not advance.

"Why did you use to hide your eyes when you were little?" I pushed her.

"Because I was scared," she yelled, suddenly tearful.

"What was scary?"

"I don't know," she said, crying. "I don't know. I was afraid

Sara . . . sometimes she sat so still. She was . . . I was afraid she was . . . that she would die." Ronnie sobbed. She sat crying, wiping each tear with the back of her hand as though this would prevent another from forming and falling.

After a moment she looked up at me, exhausted and confused. I helped her.

"From what Rena said, I think Sara was really depressed for a while after she came back from the Peace Corps. I think something about seeing the homeless women in the subway brought back the feelings of how it was for you during the time that Sara was so depressed."

Ronnie sat silent except for calming sobs, trying to take this in. She did not avoid my eyes as she often did during silent moments, but engaged them with a long pleading gaze.

"What?" I asked gently.

"But . . ." There seemed to be no words for what she wanted. Maybe the need she felt for comfort was the enormous need of the inarticulate toddler, watching helplessly as her mother turned to stone.

She shook her head blindly, suddenly collecting the things she had brought with her.

"I know it's time to go," I said, "but you might feel like staying a few minutes longer to talk some more about this. And you might want to call if you are feeling upset before your next session."

Ronnie nodded as she waved good-bye and departed quickly.

■　■　■

I felt guilty about letting her leave. Why had I taken a teenager into my private practice anyway? I felt angry with Jacob for referring her and angry at myself for perhaps making a premature interpretation, angry at myself for feeling the need to protect her from her own pain. Exhausted, I fell asleep quickly that night and dreamed.

■　■　■

A birdcage swings from a chain hooked to the ceiling, out of the reach of a tiger cat pacing the wooden floor beneath. I am walking toward it from afar, squinting to see the cage's inhabitant. A puffy blue-and-green parakeet hops from swing to perch to swing and I come closer to see him play. Suddenly I am flooded with guilt. This parakeet is mine, the parakeet I had as a child, the parakeet that died after I went away to college. But he's still alive! I panic—what about his food? Quickly I begin filling the bird's small dish until it overflows with seed. My God! I've forgotten to feed this bird for thirteen years! How has it survived despite my neglect? I feel chilled by my own carelessness. The parakeet chatters at me, still playing but scolding me for my long absence as I stand staring in disbelief.

The scene changes. It looks like a hallway—grim, colorless. Ronnie and I are standing together, watching wordlessly as two orderlies carry a sheet-covered body on a stretcher through a doorway. A commotion begins: many people surround the stretcher, coming from everywhere and nowhere. Some of these people look familiar, like distant cousins.

"Hey," the orderly calls in our direction, "she's not dead, she's calling you."

I startled—who does he mean, Ronnie or me?

Rena's raspy voice calls out, parting the crowd. I can see her sitting up on the stretcher, pushing the sheet back so that her arms are free, motioning to Ronnie. Ronnie looks stricken.

"How could you think I was dead?" Rena chastises her. "Don't you have faith in me?"

"But you were gone for so long," Ronnie stammers, pale.

"Always have faith, sweetheart," Rena clucks, more gently. "Don't forget, always have faith."

As she speaks, my own grandmother begins to peer around the corner of the corridor. I jump in excitement when I see her, but then I am awake and seeing only the shadow of the fan-blown curtain, the breeze blowing my grandmother's image back into the night.

■ ■ ■

Kendra wanted privacy. She announced this upon entering the room, then disappeared into the storage closet. I tried to follow, but she sat against the door, making it impossible to open without crushing her.

"Kendra," I called softly from the other side of the door, "that closet's not very safe for kids."

"I'm not a kid anymore," she answered sadly, seriously. "I already growed up."

"Oh." I thought about this for a moment. "Well, then, can I come in, too? I'm grown-up, too."

She opened the door graciously, as if welcoming me into her home, then sat down against the door again, now ensuring privacy for both of us. She sat there silently with arms folded across her chest.

"How did you get to be so grown-up today?" I asked her.

She shrugged, glancing up at me from under her furrowed brow, then retreating. I looked down. The dark closet seemed an unlikely refuge for Kendra, who usually avoided anything spooky, but today she seemed to be facing her own ghosts, confronting the haunting images of womanhood from which she could no longer hide.

"I guess what's scary about being a grown-up feels very private to you, like the scary things that happened to you and Mommy." I kept watching her as I spoke.

Kendra said nothing. She kicked a bin of small rubber dolls and knocked it from the storage shelf. Dolls spilled into the space between her open legs.

"It's dark in the closet like it was dark that day," I commented. Kendra and her mother had been molested in the dark.

Kendra did not answer, but began standing the rubber people up, working hard to balance each one on the stiff wool of the institutional carpet.

"That's the baby," she said in a low voice, pointing to the smallest doll. "That's the mama." She set them up side by side as if walking them down a street, the baby girl a couple of paces behind the mother. She pulled a toy car from the shelf.

"The car's comin', but the mother can't see it. The baby can see, but it comes too fast, before she can get her mama out the way." She zoomed the car into the mother and daughter's path and they fell to the ground.

"Then they both died," Kendra said sadly, looking up at me, "and they were bleeding, so the ambulance took them to the hospital and the doctor gave them a Band-Aid. Then they took the baby to give her away because she couldn't talk yet."

"Because she couldn't talk yet?" I questioned, puzzled.

"Yep. Because she couldn't say 'stop,' so the car hurted her and her mommy." She leaned her head against my arm, surveying the scene of multiple crimes.

I breathed deeply, dizzied by her conclusion.

"That's what the baby thinks," I affirmed, "but I think they took the baby because the mama stayed in the street too much where lots of cars can come and didn't know how to watch out for cars and didn't know how to tell the car to stop. She couldn't keep herself safe or watch out for the baby. So they gave the baby to her auntie, because the auntie could keep the baby safe."

Kendra retrieved another female doll from the pile at her feet.

"So the auntie said, 'Just forget about it, child. I'll be your mama now.' "

"But the baby couldn't forget about it," I added, "she still worried about her mama and she missed her, but she stopped talking about it. She started pretending about the things she could do when she was big so she could make sure no one hurt her that way again. She tried to be her own mama. But sometimes she had dreams that she was little again and she couldn't say 'stop' to save herself and her mama. She woke up and cried, and sometimes she got really mad at everyone and no one knew why except the baby."

Kendra maneuvered herself into my lap, nestling her face into the crook of my arm.

"I'll be the baby now," she said decisively. "You be the mama."

She lay curled up in my lap, fingering the laces of my shoes. Abruptly she rolled over to look at my face.

"Don't let no one kill me," she instructed, and then she fell asleep.

■ ■ ■

Everyone at the day-care center was building houses out of giant cardboard bricks. Each group had been given a pile of bricks, and furniture had been cleared from the center of the room to give space to this rainy-day project.

The two-year-olds, who had awakened from their naps, were

carefully stacking brick upon brick until the towers toppled to the floor. The tiny architects threw themselves into the rubble, emitting shrill giggles that pierced the dreams of their sleeping classmates, who cuddled against the noise.

The three-year-olds worked like small bricklayers, enclosing themselves in habitats whose walls rose above their heads; they stood on tiptoe, fingertips reaching as high as they could to add yet another storey to their creations.

Informed by invisible blueprints, the four-year-olds built real and imaginary dwellings complete with doors, windows, mailboxes and elevator shafts. They had learned from the story of "The Three Little Pigs" that brick houses were not supposed to fall, and became enraged at the child who was irreverent enough to cause the collapse of a building. Thus, more than one exasperated builder was shouting Qimmy's name in pleading tones as she wandered into their buildings and then proceeded out, oblivious to her own destructive impact, as if she were a ghost who expected to be able to walk through walls.

"Qimmy," I called, setting my bag down near Georgie's cage, "come here."

She approached me happily, her sweet round face framed by a yellow Peter Pan collar.

"Let's build here," I told her, walking her to the two-year-olds' area, where as much value was given to knocking down as building up.

I collected an assortment of bricks into a pile between us. I knelt down, resting my elbow on the pile.

"The kids are making houses, Qimmy. Let's see how you like to make a house."

She started to dance away, but I grabbed her arm, then held her hands in front of me.

"Let's try," I persisted.

Her elfin glow disappeared abruptly and her suddenly pouting face scowled at me. I handed her a brick and she stamped her foot in protest. She looked so angry that I expected her to throw it in my direction, but she just stood there, paralyzed.

"What's wrong, Qimmy?" I moved closer. She looked ashen, as though she had stopped breathing.

"Mommy house gone," she said softly, looking at the floor. I sat down on the floor in front of her to meet her gaze.

"What happened to Mommy's house?" I asked, now also breathless, awaiting her reply.

"The fireman chopped it with a hammer and it broke. Qimmy was coughing." Qimmy looked at my eyes with a bewildered expression as if the words had come out before she knew it, delivering a memory in spite of the clouds of smoke surrounding it.

"You're remembering when you were very little, and you and Mommy lived together in an apartment building, and there was a big fire. The fireman came to put the fire out and to take you and Mommy out of the fire. But maybe he couldn't open the door, so maybe he chopped it down with an ax."

"He broke my house," Qimmy repeated. "The toast got burnt and my mommy died." She looked very worried.

I sat her in my lap, and she sat her baby doll next to the pile of bricks that had become the fire-ravaged house.

"The house was burnt and Mommy was very scared and very sad," I said, "and so was Qimmy."

"Then Mommy and me went away to a place with a lot of doors," Qimmy said. "That door, that door, that door. But no door was Mommy's."

"Mommy had no door for a long time," I affirmed.

Qimmy said nothing else, but sat with me holding her baby, watching the other children build brick houses.

■   ■   ■

"Qimmy can't build a house," I said to Tina between bites of chocolate cake. We were meeting in her office this time, but she had brought bags full of snacks from home. The snacks had come to be an integral part of our meeting, as their appearance had been the turning point in our supervisory relationship. Before the snacks, Tina had thought I was too unconventional and I had thought she was too rigid.

"For Qimmy a house is not something you can play about casually. She gets flooded with images of her house being chopped up and disappearing into smoke. She may have no conscious images of the intact house that existed before the fire. She was so young when it happened."

"But there is some evidence of a more intact image of Opal," Tina mused, "because Qimmy said, 'the toast got burnt and my mommy died,' implying that for Qimmy, Opal was more alive at some point. And if house and mother are in some ways one and the same for Qimmy, the memory of the loss might be very significant. It might be what she has been dancing away from all these months."

"Meanwhile, she has been dancing with Opal more and more. She was furious when Opal stayed with Queeny in the hospital," I added. "She was acting out like crazy at day care."

"And Opal?" inquired Tina.

"Opal is nursing Queeny, who's in bed most of the day now. The nursing helps her fight her feelings of guilt about Queeny's overlooking the expiration date on her medication, which I think is transferential and really about her feeling guilty because she was unable to save her own mother. Opal is still Opal, but she cries and smiles sometimes, and there are more words and fewer still-life poses. I'm beginning to think that if they get Queeny's apartment, they'll make it alone together even after Queeny's gone."

"Are you still scared?" Tina asked, smiling, knowing what the answer would be. I shook my head.

"There's nothing scary about the Opal who lives in Queeny Martin's house."

"And if they don't get Queeny's apartment?" Tina ventured delicately.

I shrugged. "I don't know. At this point I don't know if Opal can build a house yet, either. I know she can't make it homeless, but who could?"

Tina nodded miserably. We'd both seen too many disasters to be more than marginally hopeful. We sat in silence.

"Ronnie knows how to build an igloo. Maybe you could start a group," Tina suggested teasingly.

"Too late," I replied. "Ronnie's igloo is melting."

■   ■   ■

"My mom said she wasn't depressed, it was just culture shock," Ronnie reported in a hollow voice.

Hmmm. Clearly Sara did not want to discuss this experience of culture shock. She had ignored three messages on her machine inviting her to come in.

"And what did you say?" I asked Ronnie.

"Nothing," she said, her voice still hollow. Her hands were folded across her chest and she was staring out the window.

"It looks like it is hard for you to be here with me today," I observed. "Maybe what happened here last week was too scary."

"She wouldn't even talk to me about it," Ronnie said bitterly, as if she had not heard me at all. Tears fell from her angry eyes.

This was only the second time I had seen anger in Ronnie's eyes. The first time had been when I pushed her to see the meaning of her dream. Now Sara had slammed the door on the value of that dream, closing Ronnie out as well.

Ronnie sat very still, crying silent tears as if stung by the slap of Sara's denial.

"I think your angry feelings need a voice," I said softly.

She jammed her hands into the empty pockets of her faded jeans, as if touching the emptiness would affirm her psychic reality in that moment.

"When I first came here," she began haltingly, "I thought something was really wrong with me. I thought I was dying or something, because I tried so hard to stop getting sick but nothing worked. Even though I took so much medicine, and even after Sara took me to the doctor, it wouldn't stop. I lay on my bed sometimes and thought about all the questions the doctors kept asking me, like exactly how did my stomach feel, was I dizzy when I woke up, and stuff like that. And I knew I couldn't give them the right answers. I could never answer because—it was weird— because it was like I couldn't remember. Like that stuff was happening to me, but I couldn't really feel it." She stopped to catch her breath.

I nodded for her to continue.

"I couldn't tell Sara. Part of me wanted to, because I thought Sara could somehow make it stop. Like my physical being belonged to her anyway, so she could control it, but I was so scared I couldn't tell her."

"What were you scared of?"

Ronnie shrugged, wiping away the traces of the tears.

"Think about the homeless women and the troll. What was scary about them?" I pursued.

"I was scared of the homeless women's eyes. I was afraid I'd see myself in there. . . ." Her voice trailed off. "I was afraid the troll would pull me under the ice." She looked up at me for help in making the connection.

"And you were scared to see Sara depressed and sitting so still. You were afraid that she was dying, and in the dream the Sara-troll tried to pull you under the ice where she was. You were trying to cross the bridge, maybe the bridge that goes from being a kid to being a teenager, but the Sara-troll tried to stop you by claiming your physical being to take care of her. And when you wouldn't let her, she got really angry and really scary-looking."

"She would have exploded and blown us all to smithereens," Ronnie added with a high-pitched, nervous giggle that released her from her true feelings.

"Well, that's a lot to be angry about and a lot to be scared of and a good reason to get sick enough to put growing up on hold for a little while," I commented.

The lightness fell away and she became instantly somber. She nodded and looked out the window.

"Sara left me alone," she said very quietly.

I watched her loneliness surround her and isolate her from me for a moment: an invisible igloo sheltering her from contact with me, protecting the image of Sara as good-enough mother even as it was fading.

"I know," I said. "Sara left you alone when you were a little girl, and she was depressed and couldn't be with you. She left you alone with your feelings. It must feel very lonely to remember that."

She nodded, crying again.

"Sara can't talk to you about it yet, but maybe Sara knew when she sent you to therapy that you would be able to talk about the way it felt, that you would remember."

Ronnie looked incredulous. "Sara doesn't know. I have to talk about it in a secret code, in a secret language of igloos and trolls so that Sara will never know."

"So that Sara will never know what?" I asked.

"How I feel," she said, as though this should have been evident.

"What would happen if she knew how you felt?"

"Then she might really die," she said in the reverent tone of a preschooler who still believed in magic. "She might really die then."

■ ■ ■

In a small, sweltering bedroom cooled by two oscillating fans, Queeny Martin lay under a lacy white coverlet made by her grandmother. Opal had propped the household supply of pillows behind Queeny's head so that she could sit up without exerting herself. She peered through glasses that were now too large for her face as she kept track of the TV soaps or studied the large-print headlines of the *Daily News* or attended to needlepoint projects begun long ago and put aside. But this afternoon Queeny had another project to occupy her keen mind and frail body: a ceremony to celebrate her adoption of Opal. We had planned to go out somewhere special to mark the occasion, but Queeny's health forbade this, forcing us to toast Queeny and Opal's new relationship in the quiet of Queeny's tiny room.

Commissioned to buy a box of cream puffs from the local bakery, I placed them on the small table next to Queeny's bed beside a pitcher of iced tea Opal had prepared.

"I want that one," Qimmy chirped, bouncing on the end of Queeny's mattress and pointing into the box. Qimmy had been dressed in a stiff, full-skirted yellow dress, but had whimpered and sweated until Queeny had eventually pulled off the dress. This left Qimmy outfitted in frilly yellow panties, white socks, Mary Janes, and yellow gingham hair ribbons.

Opal had assumed one of her motionless poses on a small wooden chair in the corner near the door. She was wearing an African-patterned sundress of a type sold by local street vendors. Her hair was no longer held captive by the ski cap, but fell into ringlets around her head and smelled of curl relaxant.

"Well, Opal," Queeny began, putting a cream puff on a plate for Qimmy, "I had in my mind to welcome you into my family by putting something in writing, but then my eyes got so that I could barely see what I put down on the paper, so we'll have to make do with this." She pulled something from a long brown envelope on her nightstand.

"This is the Martin family tree. Best see what you got yourself into now," she said, chuckling. She handed the document to Opal.

"Had it done some time ago," Queeny explained in my direction.

"Let me see," Qimmy demanded, bouncing over to Opal.

Opal was shading her eyes with one hand and holding the paper with the other. She let Qimmy climb into her lap as she stared into the tree's branches with a bewildered expression. She moved her fingers slowly over the document, reading it name by name, and when her finger rested, the bewilderment lifted and the unsmiled smile that she had been harboring for some months finally broke through.

"That's your name and mine," Opal announced to Qimmy. Qimmy clapped her hands and lay face-up on her mother's lap as if sunbathing in the sudden glow of Opal's joy.

No one spoke for a moment. Then Opal wordlessly handed the document to me. My hand trembled under the family history of Queeny Martin, the eighth of eleven children born to Isaiah and Daisy Martin in Stevens County, South Carolina. Queeny's date of birth was May 2, 1906. A year later Jessie May Martin was born. She died in 1914 at seven years of age. In June of 1909, Thomas Peter Martin was born. On December 17, 1911, Elizabeth Jean Martin was born. She died on December 18, 1911. Queeny's mother, Daisy Martin, died on the day of her youngest daughter's birth. Queeny had been five years old.

I looked up at Queeny, who saw my questions forming even through her weakened eyes.

"Now why do you think I never showed this to you before?" she admonished me. "I knew you'd be wanting to hear the whole of it, and I don't know whether the Lord plans to leave me on the earth long enough to tell the unabridged version."

I smiled at her through collecting tears. "How about just the part that explains who took care of you after your mother died?" I asked timidly. I felt a need to know where the mother in Queeny Martin came from.

Opal's smile had disappeared and she stared intently at Queeny, perhaps trying to imagine Queeny as the bereaved child she herself had once been. Qimmy had tuned out the conversation and was seeking refuge by falling asleep in her mother's lap. Queeny answered Opal's stare before answering me.

"I watched my mama die, too," Queeny said to Opal's disbelieving face. "The Lord took her while she was bringing life with every one of her ten children watching. Your mama died at your father's violent hand with you as God's only witness behind the bars of your crib. That's a burden no child should have to bear alone." She looked over at Qimmy's body, now the recipient of Opal's giant teardrops. I took a deep breath, realizing that I had been afraid to breathe while Queeny was talking. Opal's story was locked into her unconscious as surely as she, the toddler, had been locked in behind the bars of her crib. Opal had been confined to the scene of the crime until she could allow her feelings to release her. While I was sure she had overheard whispers of her own history as a child, I did not know whether she had ever actually been told the truth. I watched. Her breathing deepened by her crying, she took the story in with Queeny's tone and words in Queeny's own room. Perhaps I served as a magical charm of sorts, guarding against the insanity that she feared would envelop her if she were to fully feel her pain.

Queeny wiped her face with a cloth that Opal kept near the bed. She turned her head to face me.

"I couldn't have made it alone after my mother was gone. My daddy sharecropped and worked about fourteen hours every day just so we could eat. My sister Jessie died of typhoid, because if he stopped working to care for her we all would have starved. My older sisters nursed her, but they weren't really old enough to care for a sick child. They had a service for her in the church, and afterward an old woman by the name of Ida Campbell came home with us to see to us and never stopped seeing to us until the day she died. By that time I was eighteen years old."

For Queeny, volunteering for second motherhood at age seventy-nine was part of her heritage. Nurturing was as essential to the end of her life as death.

"So you see," Queeny said to Opal, looking skyward as if meaning for God to overhear, "everything comes out even in the end. Everything comes out the way it's supposed to be."

■ ■ ■

'Mitri was delivered by an apologetic bus driver.

"I couldn't get down that street to get them other kids," he explained. "Police had it all blocked off. There was no way to get through. Got this one here for you, though." He held up 'Mitri's hand. He had her in a wrist grip, as she had probably resisted being accompanied.

"Thank you. Sorry you had trouble," I told him, taking 'Mitri from his hand. She looked very worried.

"What do you think was happening in the street where the other kids live?" I asked her, leading her into the room. She shrugged, waving to Franny in a grown-up way.

"Maybe they takin' Maimai away 'cause her daddy use drugs," 'Mitri ventured. She went off to the shelf and got a large bin full of Lego pieces.

"You probably remember when that happened to you and Mommy," I replied. 'Mitri had been taken from her mother and had spent a short time in foster care a few months before being referred to the group. Her mother had been charged with possession of crack and there had been an investigation of the household, during which time 'Mitri was temporarily in foster placement. The home study and interview of 'Mitri had yielded insufficient evidence of neglect. 'Mitri was well dressed and well fed, and her home well tended, unlike many other children of crack-using women. She had been referred to treatment instead, due to her rages while in foster care.

"I remember. I bit that old woman so that they let me go home," she recalled in a self-satisfied way, snapping multicolored towers of Lego onto a solid base.

"I guess you were scared that they weren't going to let you go home," I reflected, "but do you remember what the foster mother did that made you get angry and bite her?"

"She tried to wash me," 'Mitri said matter-of-factly, "like I was a baby. I ain't no baby." She knitted her eyebrows and pouted the last words with a borrowed expression.

"You weren't a baby," I agreed, "but I think you were very scared, because if you weren't so scared you could have said, 'I like to take a bath by myself,' instead of biting."

'Mitri said nothing, but snapped a roof onto her construction, a windowless house. She popped a Lego person in through the only door.

"That's a crack house," she said with certainty. She shook it so that the small person rattled against the walls.

"Sounds like she's all alone in there," I observed.

"She is. It's all smoky and there ain't no bathtub."

"Uh-oh. How does she get clean, then?" I inquired.

"She don't. She just think she clean, but she ain't really. Crack house is all make-believe," she observed coolly, looking at me with resentful eyes.

This was a chilling observation, explaining why children's make-believe play was so frightening to 'Mitri.

"What else do they make-believe in a crack house, 'Mitri?"

'Mitri gave her characteristic shrug in response, then continued her play.

"They makin' believe they all eatin' chocolate candy and they feel good. They makin' believe they rich people and they don't got no kids."

"But that little girl is a kid. Whose little girl is she?"

"She's a little girl, but she making' believe she the watch guard, all 'cause they always think somebody's comin' and then they be in jail. But nobody do come, mostly," she added with some regret.

"Nobody comes and then the little girl can't stop the make-believe and she feels afraid, but if somebody comes they might take the little girl away. Then what will happen?"

"Then there won't be no guard," 'Mitri said, as though this should have been obvious.

"Well, what if there was another guard so the girl didn't have to worry about that?"

'Mitri said nothing, but began working on another house. "Then she be cryin' like a baby," she said finally, emphatically.

"Why?"

" 'Cause she be so hungry, cause she just ate make-believe food for a hundred days," 'Mitri said, this time with hungry eyes, "and she couldn't get any real food."

"She couldn't get any real food even in foster care?" I asked.

"She don't know," 'Mitri said again, exasperated with me. "She didn't know *then,* anyhow," she added after a moment, " 'cause she never ate no graham crackers before, so she didn't know what kind of stuff she might get."

"She didn't know what kind of stuff she might get in foster care," I repeated. "She didn't know if she would get good food like graham crackers or whether it would be make-believe food again. It's a hard decision for a little girl to make, because being a guard means having to keep the adults that she loves safe and not letting anyone know what's really happening. Not letting anyone know that she's really hungry. That's a scary story."

'Mitri rolled her eyes. "Franny," she called, "tell Lesley don't be scared."

"Nope," Franny said, "I'll tell her it's all right to be scared here."

"You two act crazy," 'Mitri concluded, taking the juice and graham crackers that Franny handed to her and dropping her newly constructed house with windows next to the windowless crack house in the bin.

■ ■ ■

Franklyn reached me at the clinic.

"Sorry to bother you on your other job, but I have good news. Opal States got an apartment."

I was silent, stunned. "What? Where?"

"In Brooklyn, Bedford-Stuyvesant. One-bedroom city housing with special services on site for tenants who are coming from homeless shelters and, in this case, for Opal."

I recovered somewhat. "But Franklyn, she's doing great where she is."

"I know that, but what happens after Queeny goes and she

applies to Housing and is turned down? I can't advise that. She can't wait on that chance when she's got a sure thing here."

I felt panicky. It was the end of July. I was going to Vermont in one week and had no time to . . . to do what?

"When would she need to move?" I asked finally, dizzy.

"September first."

How would she cope in an unfamiliar neighborhood without Queeny? I thought. "Queeny! What about Queeny? She's dependent on Opal for care at this point."

"Opal can still care for Queeny during the day while Qimmy is at the day-care center. That way no one has to make any radical changes. If Queeny needs evening care, well, we'll request a home attendant for her. Are you there?"

"Yeah, sorry. I know you're right, it's good news, but . . . unexpected."

"Well, if you put your name on a waiting list for long enough, your turn will come."

"Yeah, right." I realized it had been exactly one year since Betsy had summoned me to the day-care center to talk to Opal States. Her name had gone on a list for city housing six months before that.

"I'll go out to Mrs. Martin's apartment tomorrow morning to tell Mrs. Martin and Opal. Would you like to be there?"

"I can't. I have an appointment at a school district in the Bronx tomorrow morning." I had to try to convince the district that served my group patients to allow group to continue for another month after school began again, although the original contract had been for only one year. We needed to extend the time to leave the girls with a "safe image" during the vacation month ahead.

"Okay, then. One more thing. The court is requesting a letter from you commenting on Opal's ability to care for Qimmy in order for us to release her from Mrs. Martin's care. Can you give me something?"

"Yeah," I heard myself say. "With mandated services, I can recommend that Qimmy be released to Opal."

"All right. We want to move on this quickly to help Opal take the steps she needs to secure the apartment."

"Right," I said, struggling to believe that something good was happening.

Franklyn breathed a sigh of relief. "Compared to what else I've got here, this case is starting to look like a shining star in my case load. No one's crack-addicted. Qimmy's in a program. Opal's got housing. You can't hope for much more."

In fact, Opal had much more than what Franklyn had named. Opal had feelings of connection, and those feelings might indeed allow her to succeed in the transformation from subway-dweller to subway commuter that Franklyn envisioned.

"She may be afraid. She'll need you to stay involved even after she's got her own place. Will you still be the Preventive Services worker at that point?" I asked hopefully.

"I'll talk to my supervisor. Will you still be at the day-care center?"

"I'll be around," I promised, not really knowing what Betsy had in mind for the coming year.

I suddenly felt very connected to Franklyn. It was as though we realized, at that moment, that we were virtually related and suddenly threatened by an institutional annulment. We said good-bye, promising to talk again before I left for vacation.

■ ■ ■

"Guess what this is?" Ronnie bubbled, holding an envelope addressed to her.

"What?" I asked playfully.

"A letter from my dad. Look!" She pulled it from the envelope and laid it in my lap, beaming as I glanced at it.

"How did this happen?" I asked, surprised.

"I copied the return address off the child support envelope a long time ago, so finally I asked Sara if I could write to him and she said yes and he answered me." Ronnie sounded surprised, too. "Look," she said, pointing to the return address, "he lives in Seattle."

I looked at the address and the letter, a short note acknowledging Ronnie's card and expressing joy that she had sought him out.

"I'm going to write back and send him a picture of me and ask for a picture of him," she said jubilantly. "Maybe I look like him"—she giggled shyly—"but everyone says I look like Rena—uh-oh."

She gave me a winning look, pleading and guilty at the same time.

"What?"

"I forgot to tell you Rena is taking the second half of my session today because I am going to an end-of-the-summer party for counselors-in-training. Is that okay?"

Ronnie had a summer job at a YMHA day camp.

"It would be nice if we had talked about it, especially since this is the last session before my vacation," I reminded her, not quite ready to let her off the hook.

"Sorry," she said sweetly, adding, "Oh—Sara wants to know how long you will be gone."

"Three weeks."

"Oh yeah, I forgot."

"And what do you want to know?" I asked, doubting that Sara had much interest in the length of my vacation.

"I want to know where you'll be," she said hurriedly.

"You want me to call you during that time to see how you're doing?" I offered.

She shook her head. "That's okay. I just want you to tell me where you'll be. I just want to picture you somewhere."

"Oh," I said, understanding. "I'll be in Vermont."

"What will it look like where you are staying?" she persisted.

"Remember once you told me you went to Vermont when you were little? What was it like?" I inquired.

She looked at the ceiling. "Long, bumpy roads with no streetlights," she recalled slowly, "hills with so many trees they looked like broccoli from far away." She giggled at this for a minute. "And excellent little stores. One time the man at the store in my cousin's town let me taste three kinds of maple candy."

I smiled at her memories.

"I'll picture you at the store," she concluded. Then, "I hope I don't dream about you."

"Why?" I wondered, feeling slightly rejected.

" 'Cause in real life I know that nothing will happen to you while you are away, but in the dream it might."

"I think you're worried something could happen in real life. That's why it comes up in your dreams. I wonder if getting the letter from your dad made you worry about me somehow," I ventured.

"No," she said quickly, annoyed at my interpretation. "Anyways, I'll be gone, too, part of the time you're away," she said, as though I had not spoken. "I'm going with my friend Cindy and her family."

"Where will you be?" I asked. "That way I can picture you."

She loved this idea and gave me a glowing smile that could probably be seen in Vermont. "Fire Island. And it looks like the beach, in case you don't know."

I nodded. "Okay. I'll picture you at the beach. We can talk some more about your dad's letter when we both come back."

Ronnie nodded and began to collect her things. "I forgot to leave the door open for Rena," she recalled. It was impossible to hear my doorbell when the treatment room door was closed. "I'll go check. If she's not here yet, I'll be back."

I knew Rena would be waiting. I knew Ronnie's plan was in part an avoidance of our separation. "Come back and say good-bye even if Rena's there," I called out to her.

"Good-bye," she called out from the other room.

Rena entered and took my hand in greeting.

"Ah," she said gesturing toward the working air conditioner. "I said to myself on the train on the way over, 'At least if I have to tell about my family troubles, it should be in a comfortable room.'" She eased into a butterfly chair, her face contorted perhaps by her effort to be courteous and sociable while fearing the retelling of painful times.

"Ronnie asked me why Sara was depressed," she began immediately. "It seems that Sara herself cannot remember. Well, I think it's better I tell you the facts of what I know than to tell Ronnie. After all, she is still a child. This way you can give her what will help her and keep the rest between us."

I nodded, more to indicate that I was following her than to

express agreement, as I wasn't yet certain what I was going to hear.

"This is a way I think I made a mistake with Sara," she continued. I shook my head slightly, not understanding. "I mean, maybe with Sara I told too many facts, too much too soon. I didn't realize, maybe, the notions a child takes into her head, and my husband Max, he should rest in peace, was a talkative man also."

"What do you think you talked about too early?" I inquired.

"We were children in Europe, Max and I, before the war, in very hard times for the Jews. Everyone knew it would get worse. Everyone knew the Germans were getting closer." Rena stopped for a moment to swallow the fear that was creeping into her voice and bringing drops of sweat to her forehead in spite of the air-conditioning.

"Everyone knew, but they could do nothing. We could only wait and worry. But my mother was a very resourceful woman. My mother was a woman of action. She knew a neighbor whose last name was the same as ours who had rich relatives in New York. The neighbors' relatives sent for the neighbors' children and booked passage on a ship for them to America, to keep them safe until the war was over. But one of the children developed a sickness at the last minute and was not able to travel. My mother convinced the neighbor to allow me to go in the ill child's place. At least the other daughter would not be alone in the journey. I was very fortunate," she added, her voice trembling with bitterness.

"It doesn't sound like you felt fortunate," I said.

"As a child, only fourteen years old, pushed by my mother to leave my home? What did I know? Only that I wanted my parents to come with me. I screamed so hard when the neighbor came to take me to the ship that my father slapped me." Her eyes filled, but the tears did not spill. "I became a woman on that ship," she said softly, looking suddenly at the weaving of her straw bag.

"You mean being so suddenly on your own?" I was not sure I understood.

"I mean I had my first menstruation. I saw blood and I thought it meant I would die and I would never see my mother.

I became completely withdrawn. They thought I was sick from the sea, but I was sick from fear and grief. I didn't know," she said sadly, "that it would be my parents who died at the hands of a murderer. Their blood and not my own." The tears finally spilled, washing away the face-lift, unmasking the carving with its lines made deep by the tears of grief cried in childhood, shed too far from any source of comfort. No one had been there to prevent the scars from forming.

I offered her a tissue, which she took. I sat for a moment awash in her pain, the pain of my own grandparents and great-grandparents who had shared the same fate as her parents.

Rena dabbed her tears and continued. "Max was not so fortunate. He was from Hungary and did not get out until he was an adult. He saw terrible things there, the blood of Jewish children spilled. This is a phrase he would use in the house with Sara when she was a little girl. She would run and be careless about where she left her toys and trip and fall sometimes. He would rage at her, 'Look what you're doing! You don't watch out for yourself. Who will watch out for you? They spilled the blood of Jewish children in Europe with no one left to look out for them!' "

She drew in her breath sharply. "It was terrible. I should have stopped him maybe, but we were not educated people. I didn't know so much when I was young, and Max was a good man. He thought maybe he could protect Sara this way. I don't know." She stopped talking and looked puzzled. "It's funny. I didn't think I would tell you all this. I thought I would be talking about what happened to Sara when she came home from the Peace Corps, but instead I am thinking about Sara when she was a child like Ronnie."

"Maybe what happened when Sara was young was also important later," I offered. She nodded, sitting somber and pensive. "When did Sara get her period?"

"She was also fourteen, like myself."

And like Ronnie, I thought.

"She was frightened and started to have nightmares around that time. I didn't understand it, but something was wrong. Maybe not so much with her; after all, she was a child. But maybe with me. I felt nervous all of a sudden. I felt afraid when she left the house. Max told me, 'Rena, please. By now Sara is watching out for herself, and she is a careful girl.' So I didn't tell Sara my fears." Rena looked at me, wanting something.

"You didn't want her to know that you were afraid. Does Sara know the story of how you lost your mother?"

Rena shook her head. "Yes and no. I mean, it was like I didn't know it myself anymore. Believe it or not, by that time I felt that my life before I came to America belonged to somebody else. I knew the facts and I told the facts to Sara, but I told them like I had never been a teenager myself."

"You knew the facts, but somehow the feelings started to come back with Sara's adolescence, and that must have been what was so terrifying to both of you."

Rena's tears returned. "We were both depressed, I think. Sara had become very withdrawn, and I would push her to be social so I didn't have to see her sad face. When the Peace Corps took her I felt relief from my fears. My husband thought that my fears would get worse, but they got better." She shrugged. "Who knows how the human mind works?"

"For you it seemed that with Sara gone the fears could go back into hiding."

Rena agreed with a vigorous nod. "But when she came back, it was she who could not escape from the fears. I didn't feel afraid anymore. We had Ronnie, and she was beautiful and strong and smart. I felt hopeful and I wanted Sara to feel hopeful, too, but maybe that was a mistake. Maybe she needed our permission to feel the fears we were not brave enough to feel. Maybe she thought she had to end her life because she could not escape those feelings the way we seemed to. She could not banish them." Rena sniffed and took a breath. "Now it is Sara who refuses to feel. It is she who has forgotten, and by now I don't think she will ever remember, even for her daughter."

"Maybe it is not too late to give her your permission," I suggested quietly.

Rena looked doubtful. "Maybe when Sara has a grandchild to hold she will feel . . ."

I continued for her, "She will feel . . . ?"

"Hopeful," said Rena. Then, "Oh. I see that I am still not ready yet to give this permission."

"It's not so easy," I commented.

"It's not so easy," she agreed.

HOUSE
WARMING

I had given myself permission to be without them. As I drove down long, bumpy roads without any streetlights, looking at hillsides full of trees that looked like broccoli, in the company of friends who had known me through my own belated adolescence, I felt surrounded by time. Every day there was time to wake up slowly, to watch the clouds decide what the day's weather would be, to discover a pond that was clear and wonderful for swimming, and to watch the fire turn to embers in the stone fireplace. Without the demands of daily contact with my patients, there was time for my own fantasies to play outside of the usual analytic hour. There was time to contemplate the wish for a reality that allowed them to flourish in my daily life.

At night, countertransferential images shadowed my dreams and I saw Ronnie in a room full of different shapes and sizes of tampons, afraid and crying. I saw Opal wandering from apartment to apartment in a giant housing project, desperately searching for the door that was her own. I saw Maimai watch open-mouthed as her baby doll was lowered into the ground in a wooden box.

I saw myself standing in a field of wildflowers. It was my job to build a road spanning the field without crushing any of the flowers. I was certain there must be some way to do this, and I stood thinking. I was then transported to a large sunny room with many children in the care of a few adults.

"You should remember their names from last time," I was told, but I had never seen these children before. They all looked damaged in some way, but they were able to talk. I asked each to tell me his name.

"Kitchen floor," one shouted.

"Bathtub," another answered.

I looked to the adults for explanation.

"They are named after the places where they got hurt," a man told me. "This boy fell on his kitchen floor and was injured, so that became his name."

A woman with long blond hair began passing out candles, one to each child. "They can't be allowed to light them," she told me sternly. "Children should never be trusted with candles."

Why was she giving them candles? I wondered. "But it's Hanukkah," I protested suddenly, only realizing at that moment that it was. "They can all put their candles in the menorah and watch them burn down together. We'll be here, too."

The blond woman said, "Oh! We didn't know these children were Jewish," and graciously produced a giant silver menorah, large enough to accommodate the children's dinner-sized candles lit with giant matches. Everyone was silent in the sudden darkness.

In another dark place, Maimai's silhouette danced against the walls of a shack illuminated by a cone of sunlight that had pushed its way through a breathing space in the rotting wood. Maimai was raising her hand wildly, as if desperate to ask permission for something. A female silhouette a few feet away from her nodded. Maimai pushed open the wooden door and ran out into the sun wearing no clothes or shoes, as if she knew she did not need them. She ran to a rock in the middle of a grassy meadow and sat down. She began to pee, smiling broadly as she watched herself wetting the rock, knowing that the river came from her, having gotten the permission she needed to feel her feelings, to know what was her own. A larger rush of water came from behind, mixed with hers, and carried her from the rock but did not pull her under. Instead, it circled her like a giant whirlpool bath, washing over the tiny house in the meadow and then subsiding, leaving everything clean and glistening.

There was a painting of an igloo on the wall above a fireplace. A small fire curled around a single log, burning silently. The painting in its heavy wooden frame pulled from the hook; it hung as if leaning over for a view of the fire. The flames rose around the log and sent sparks and popping sounds like firecrackers up into the flue, which pulled the fire toward it with a whoosh, causing the flames to jump into a blaze. Waves of heat blurred the igloo and the blue sky behind it until the white of the paint became the white of snow and the snow became icy water in the heat, first dripping, then pouring into the fire, threatening the life of the flames as the flames threatened the structure of the igloo.

I opened my eyes, eager for a better view of the conflict between the ice and the fire, but they were gone, displaced by green Vermont hills dotted by clouds still asleep on the treetops, resisting the morning.

■ ■ ■

"My mama said we're not comin' back here no more," Raquel said casually as the little girls pulled off their new-school-year sweaters. Maimai and 'Mitri froze with their fingers on the stiff buttons, caught by the impossibility of reunion and departure in the same moment. Angie spilled her bag of Red Hots, which went bouncing in the silence in the room. Kendra kept unbuttoning, but looked tearful.

I glanced at Franny. We were ready to bring up the issue of termination today, but hadn't planned to do it the moment they walked through the door. We had gotten permission from the school district to extend our prevention group one month into the girls' first-grade year. After that the district believed that a morning group would interfere with academics and thus cause the failure we all hoped to prevent. Franny and I would refer the kids to the clinic for continuing individual treatment that could be scheduled after school. Then we would wait a few months to receive more at-risk kindergarten referrals from the district.

"We're coming back again," I said. "We're coming back two

times a week until September is finished. That's eight times we have to work together and say good-bye to each other. Look, Franny can show you on the calendar."

The girls gathered around to see the picture of a waving hand on the calendar, designed to depict termination at the end of the month.

"Why?" Kendra asked uncomprehendingly. Her auburn-colored hair had been gathered into a bun on top of her head. She wore a frilly white dress with hearts across the front.

"Because if we keep working together in the morning, you will miss a lot of schoolwork and it will be hard to catch up," I explained, "and because you have all gotten better at knowing how to be friends with each other and at having friends in school, and that's one of the things that the group is for."

"Maimai don't pee on herself no more," 'Mitri said thoughtfully, "and Kendra don't cry too much."

"Yeah, but Angie's still grabbin' things that don't belong to her," Raquel said in an accusing tone. Angie said nothing, but pouted charmingly.

"Everybody who still needs therapy will see a therapist at the clinic. Everyone will still be able to play with someone about the things that are important to them." I was trying to sound convincing to myself as well as to them. Some of them would be in my own patient load, but I didn't yet know how many hours I would have.

"Then you and Franny will live here all by yourself." Angie gasped, concerned at this prospect.

"You think Lesley and I live here, Angie?" Franny asked. Angie nodded seriously.

"You dumb-dumb," 'Mitri said impatiently. "Where you think they sleep?"

Angie pointed to the pile of pillows that constituted our soft corner.

"Well, where you think they eat, then?" 'Mitri challenged.

"There," Angie said, pointing to the house corner.

"But that ain't real food, do-do, that's make-believe," yelled 'Mitri, becoming agitated.

"That's real when we go home," Angie said, unperturbed by 'Mitri's reaction.

The quality of Angie's thinking disturbed me. I couldn't tell whether she was just desperate to maintain her fantasy of Franny and me as inseparable parents, or whether there was truly a psychotic stream in her thinking.

"How could the food get to be real when you go home?" I asked.

"For you to eat," she persisted, without further elaboration.

Hmmm. The concept of the group dissipating was disintegrating Angie.

"Franny and I will still be at the clinic even when we finish the group, and we'll see you when you come to the clinic for therapy after school," I told her. She gave no indication of hearing me, but skipped to the other side of the room, where she began preparing either real or make-believe plastic food.

Kendra quietly slipped her new loose-leaf notebook from her school bag and showed it to Franny. "I have a notebook this year, Franny, 'cause I'm in first grade," she said proudly.

"Yeah, me too," said Maimai emphatically, "but my room ain't got painting or baby dolls neither, not like this room."

"I know!" said 'Mitri, taking the paintbrush from the easel in hand. "You could get a note from welfare. Tell them we all crazy and we need to come here every day, not just after school."

This was the first time the issue of "being crazy" had come up.

"We ain't crazy," said Raquel quickly, looking at Franny and me with a worried expression.

"What does it mean to be crazy?" I asked, lying against the pillows Angie had designated as my bed.

"Like we be when we scream all the time," 'Mitri said as if talking to a child.

"Like when we think Freddy Kruger be in the bathroom and he ain't there," Maimai added, jumping up and down on a pillow next to me as if it were a trampoline. At that moment Raquel ran over and pulled the pillow from beneath Maimai's feet, and they both fell into the pillow pile, resulting in a chorus of anxious giggles.

"I'm not crazy in my school," Kendra asserted. "I don't cry when I go there."

"I don't cry when I go there, either," 'Mitri replied. "I only cry here."

I heard real sadness in 'Mitri's voice, and I looked up to see her paintbrush fall and her face fold into sobs.

"Come here." I held my arm out, and 'Mitri came into my lap to cry. " 'Mitri is very sad about the group ending. I think she is afraid there will be nowhere to cry when we say good-bye. She's never been in individual therapy before, so she's not sure that's a good place to cry even though we know that it is." I struggled to interpret over her noisy sobs and choking gasps.

"I have to pee," Maimai said, looking stricken.

"Come on, Maimai," Franny offered. "I'll take you."

"Me too," chimed Raquel and Kendra, eager for relief from 'Mitri's tears. They followed Franny out of the room as 'Mitri continued to cry in my arms.

"Look what I can do." I was startled by a strange tone of voice from across the room. I looked up to glimpse Angie standing precariously on top of a tall toy cabinet, apparently having climbed up by way of the open shelves. She was reaching for the fluorescent light fixtures attached to the ceiling. I scrambled to her, rolling 'Mitri onto the pillows.

"Angie, come down," I said firmly. I could not reach her; she was too high. Besides, the cabinet shelves would not have held my weight.

"I'm going to swing," she said in an odd singsong voice.

"No, Angie, that's too dangerous. The lights are not strong enough to hold a little girl. You'll fall down and get hurt. Now sit down so I can reach your feet and help you get off." I heard my voice shake. She was in danger.

"I won't get hurt," she said, standing on tiptoe and leaning farther. "I joined the circus."

"You are in group and are upset about having to say good-bye to the group. Maybe you think we are sending you away, that we don't want you anymore, and you're pretending to join the circus and go far, far away from us. We're still here and you need to come down and talk to us."

Angie stood still for a minute, her chubby hands at her sides and her eyes shining oddly and unfocused. "I can swing," she said again, this time jumping slightly.

I pushed a table beside the cabinet, then lifted a chair on top of it and climbed up to catch her feet. She reached in the direction of the fixture and tried to kick my hands away.

"I want to swing," she insisted, and kicked harder, wrenching her foot away from my grasp.

I jumped enough to reach behind her and slapped her bottom. "Sit down," I yelled. She collapsed in a crying heap on top of the cabinet. I pulled her onto the chair and then lifted her to the ground as she flailed and scratched at me. I was trembling; 'Mitri was still crying softly, and Angie was wailing.

"That hurt you," I said, holding her from behind, "because you are a real kid and you feel things. You are not in the circus. You are a little girl and you are here and you would have gotten really hurt if you had tried to swing and fell down."

Angie continued to cry, but she stopped battling me and leaned her chubby body against my chest. 'Mitri had fallen asleep in the pillows.

This was day one of our group good-bye.

■ ■ ■

"I scheduled Angie for a psychiatric and began seeing her individually to bridge the transition," I told Tina after a detailed account of our first day back.

"She feels so dispensable and her reality testing is so poor. I don't know if you're going to be able to keep her safe through this," Tina said with concern. The unspoken implication here was the hospital.

"I know," I said quietly. "I'm going to ask Jonathan what he thinks." Jonathan was the clinic psychiatrist. "Maybe day treatment is the answer." I hoped this might be the solution for Angie: a day-school program in a clinical setting.

Tina nodded. We sat there for a minute letting the leafy trees in Tina's backyard shade us from the reality of Angie's psychotic behavior.

I thought about my Vermont dreams, as they summarized the themes of my case load: mothers and daughters striving to

maintain connection with permission to feel their own feelings. If
that early connection was broken, or was maintained at the cost
of emotional surrender, development suffered. Children need to
know that their feelings will not annihilate the parent, that the
heat of their emotions won't melt and destroy the igloo, that the
igloo will not turn into an icy, raging, drowning river in retaliation. Both mother and daughter needed to tolerate the conflicts
that permission to feel engenders. Ronnie struggled to keep these
conflicts alive, filling in generation gaps with connective tissue
from her unconscious, so that the bonds among her and Rena
and Sara could survive the separation of adolescence. Opal and
Qimmy struggled to nurture their newfound connection so that
it would be strong enough for conflict to occur. But Angie hadn't
had Queeny Martin as an emotional wetnurse and had no real,
available mother or father in infancy or toddlerhood to recall
while in therapeutic arms.

"Even the group couldn't hold her," Tina reflected.

"It only provided a kind of temporary glue. The other kids
used each other like the little lost boys used each other in *Peter
Pan.* There was a group identity; the little lost girls. Franny and
I were endowed with the same kind of magic that Peter had given
Wendy. But Angie could never acknowledge her reality as an
abandoned child," I said sadly. "So she could never connect to
others who shared her reality."

"Well, isn't part of what we wanted from this group diagnos-
tic clarity for kids with multiple traumas and deprivations?" Tina
asked with professional perspective.

I nodded miserably, wishing I was the supervisor in this case
instead of the clinician, so that I would have a clinical perspective
without feeling I was losing Angie to a traveling circus.

■ ■ ■

"Hi," Ronnie panted, looking at her watch as she plopped into
her favorite butterfly chair. "I thought I was going to be really
late."

I looked at my watch. It was a couple of minutes later than
her session usually began.

"Hi," I said, smiling at her. "Last I saw you, you were saying good-bye on your way out of a very short session. And today you thought you were going to cut it short on the other end."

"God! That was so many weeks ago!" she responded in an exaggerated teenage tone. "I didn't even remember. How was Vermont?"

"Nice," I answered. "How about Fire Island?"

She smiled shyly, an "I'm hiding something" smile. "It was okay." She pulled on the end of her pocket zipper. "You know."

"I'm not sure if I know, because you're not telling me anything," I pointed out.

She giggled. "Sara said Fire Island is a scene. You know."

"Well, what kind of a scene was it when you were there?" I asked.

"Well, Cindy's whole family came for a cookout and she has all of these cousins—boys, I mean—and they were acting *so* weird. This one named Daniel kept telling me I looked like someone he saw on a music video." She giggled again.

"How did he look to you?" I wondered.

She shrugged. "Nice, like a kid, you know."

This "you know" stuff could get old fast, I thought. Then I thought, she really is being a teenager. I'm finally treating the teenager in Ronnie instead of the child taking over the role of parent.

"Guess what I got while you were gone?" she asked, smiling widely while rummaging for something in her purse. "That's *him,*" she said, handing me a photograph.

Ronnie's father had red hair like hers and Rena's. He had bushy eyebrows and a woolly beard that gave him a woodsman-like presence. His cheekbones and hairline were Ronnie's. He stood shading his eyes from the sun, looking across a mountain range.

"What do you think?" I asked her.

She shrugged again. "I don't know. It feels funny." She looked depressed, as though she were fighting a feeling that wasn't at all funny. "I was so excited when the picture came. I was so happy that he had red hair like me, but after a few days it got to be . . . I don't know, just a picture."

"When did it come?" I asked her.

"Before I went to Cindy's after you went to Vermont." She looked down at the now invisible photograph enclosed in the envelope.

"I had scary dreams while you were away." She gave me a blaming look.

"What were they?"

She said nothing but kept looking down.

"Did bad things happen to me in the dreams?" I asked her, trying to peer under her closed lashes.

"How did you know that?" she asked, disarmed, regarding me as if I were magical.

"Intuition," I answered, "and I remembered that you were afraid about that."

"Well, do you know what *happened* to you in my dream?" she continued as if under a spell.

I shook my head. "Tell me."

"When I went to see you, there were all these fire trucks in front of your building and I told the doorman I was going up to 10-B and he said, no, there was a fire there and I couldn't go in. I started crying, saying that I had an appointment. He kept saying 'Nothing we can do,' so I started ringing the buzzer from the lobby, but you didn't answer and the fireman said, 'She can't answer that where she is,' and I woke up really fast and turned on the light." She looked relieved, less spellbound.

"You figured when he said, 'She can't answer that where she is,' he meant I was dead?"

"I figured he meant that you were dead, but I knew that you were really in Vermont, but all of a sudden I wasn't sure, so I had to wake up."

"And when you woke up?"

"I was scared, but once the light was on I said to myself, 'She's really in Vermont.' Sara saw the light and asked if I was all right."

"What did you say?"

"I said yes and then I went back to sleep, and I woke up in the morning and I went to look at my dad's picture, but it felt weird. When I first got it the picture made him seem like a real person, then he changed back to just a picture. It felt creepy."

"What do you think made him feel real when you first got it?"

Ronnie squinted, trying to retrieve the daddy image she had had for a few days. "Me," she said finally. "I mean, I started thinking about what he would be like, like if he came here, what we would do. You know, things like that."

"And then?"

"And then he just started looking like a stranger. Like how can I imagine doing things with this man? I don't even know him."

"Maybe you got scared," I proposed. "In your head you were getting to know him and maybe beginning to like him, and maybe you got scared it would hurt Sara too much and maybe hurt me in some way, too."

"Can you talk to Sara about it?" Ronnie asked suddenly, surprising me, as I had expected denial.

I would love to talk to Sara about it, as well as about a few hundred other things, I thought.

"Do you think that would help?" I managed to ask.

She nodded. "Talking does help, I decided," she said emphatically. "Remember when Sara and I first came and I said, 'Am I just supposed to talk to you?' Sara didn't believe it would work, either. She thought I should take medication or something. Now I believe it, but Sara doesn't really."

"And you are wondering if we can make Sara a believer?"

Ronnie nodded. "We can," she said with certainty, needing to believe that Sara could accept comfort for the hurt of Ronnie's emerging as a young woman, separate from her mother. "We can for sure."

■ ■ ■

"Ronnie wanted me to come," Sara said hurriedly, by way of explanation as I opened the front door. "I know I don't have an appointment, but I've been so busy, I thought I'd drop by on my way home and see by chance if you would take a few minutes to talk to me." She was shaking out her wet umbrella in the hallway as we spoke, not really looking at me.

I considered whether to send her home with an appointment card, then concluded that it might be now or never.

"Come in," I said, hoping I still looked somewhat professional after a long day that included Qimmy's paints and a group project of making play dough. We went into the office and sat down. I looked at Sara and saw that she too had given all of herself to her day. Her hair pulled away from the barrette and her face looked worn. We were both wearing full denim skirts and looked like a set of bookends, each weary from holding up the corner of the world that we imagined would collapse without us.

"I know it has been a long time," Sara said apologetically. "You probably wondered if Ronnie had become an orphan," she added with sarcasm.

"I was hoping that her gaining one parent didn't mean she was losing the other." I looked into Sara's brown eyes for feeling.

"Oh, you mean Rick? I told Ronnie it was okay for her to contact him," she said in a high voice. "I've been reading some about the adolescent need for identity figures. Ronnie's very motivated and she knows I won't stand in the way of her getting to know her father."

"She knows you won't stand in her way, but I'm not sure she knows how you're feeling about it. She was worried about that," I added.

Sara looked surprised. "Really? She seems so self-absorbed lately. I'm surprised. Well, I feel fine about it. I just hope she doesn't get too invested in the whole thing. I mean, I'm not sure how committed he would be. . . ." Her voice trailed off.

"I know you don't want her to get hurt," I said, "but I think she is worried about your getting hurt if she gets to know Rick."

Sara brightened. "We're worried about each other, then," she said, seeming comforted.

"I know, but as you say, teenagers have a need for identity figures, and I'm afraid that if Ronnie stays worried she won't let herself find hers."

Sara looked exhausted. "She has nothing to worry about really," she said in an emotionless voice. Then, "I would never cut myself off from Ronnie." This was said with genuine feeling.

The problem is, I thought, that if you cut yourself off from yourself, it is impossible to be there for someone else. I waited.

"I know my mother has been coming to see you. I'm not sure what she has been telling you, but I'm glad she has someone to talk to. I don't think she ever recovered from my teenage years. She seems to be thinking about the past a lot. I read that that's a sign of aging, although it's hard to think of my mother as an old woman." Sara rolled her eyes. I nodded. "I had a difficult adolescence. I must have given them a lot of grief." There was guilt in her voice and in her eyes. "So I'm glad my mother can talk about it now. That way I don't have to feel so much guilt," she said, her voice brightening.

"Maybe they gave you a lot of grief in childhood," I proposed, now feeling guilt myself because I knew more than she might assume.

"Maybe," Sara said airily. "I don't remember much. I've been blessed with a very short memory. That way I don't dwell on the past."

No, I thought, that way, instead, the past dwells in you, preventing you from feeling, preventing you from giving your child your blessing to grow up, robbing you of the chance to bear witness to the miracle of her growth.

■　■　■

"Greetings," said Betsy heartily, "welcome to chaos in the making." She made a sweeping gesture. There was the sound of weeping from the two-year-old group in their first month of day care, a clattering crew of workmen repairing the overhead pipes, which were supposed to have been fixed during the center's two-week break, and a shape search going on in the four-year-old group which had children scrambling all over the center to claim any items that were circular.

I smiled. "You love chaos," I reminded her.

"Oh, yeah, right," she said. "Looking for your big girl? She seems very grown-up to me these days compared to these new little people we have running around here."

"How is she?" I asked quickly. I hadn't seen Qimmy or Opal since their move to Brooklyn during my vacation.

Betsy dragged on a plastic cigarette. "All in all," she said, responding slowly to keep me on the edge of my seat, "I think Qimmy is doing pretty well. For the first couple of weeks she cried a lot, had low frustration tolerance, and slept most of the afternoon. Opal looked drained when she came in the morning. I couldn't get her to hang around much because she had to go to Queeny. She'd come back at four o'clock to pick Qimmy up, because that's when the home attendant would arrive. I don't think Opal liked being around when the woman was there, so that meant Qimmy never got to see Queeny and I think that was distressing to her. So we got Opal to pick Qimmy up for lunch and take her to Queeny's and then bring her back to school for the afternoon. Qimmy has been better since then."

"That was brilliant," I commented.

"Thank you," Betsy said, delighted. "By the way, the big W question has come into play. It's wonderful, cognitively speaking, I mean."

I laughed. "Oh, you mean I should get ready for 'Why are you wearing those earrings?' "

Betsy nodded, simultaneously picking up the phone.

Qimmy was standing on a chair to reach a doll dish on top of the shelf. She jumped down when she saw me and ran to give me a hug.

"Hi!" I was happy to see her, too.

"Why you went away?" she asked solemnly.

I was stumped for a moment. This was a "why" question I didn't think she would be capable of asking so soon.

"I went away on vacation," I told her, kneeling down to see her face. "A vacation means having time to play. Then I came back and now I can see you." This seemed as acceptable as anything would have been. "Maybe you missed me while I was away," I told her. "So many things happened to you and Mommy."

Qimmy said nothing, but grabbed my finger and towed me into the thick of the group to be presented to Maria. "Look," she said triumphantly.

Maria turned around. "Oh, you're back! Well, somebody will be happy. She told me you went to New Jersey."

I shook my head.

"She said, 'Lesley went to New Jersey on TV.' "

"I'm not sure where she . . . oh, wait a minute." I recalled something from a television commercial, Bill Cosby talking about taking a vacation in New Jersey. It was probably the only context Qimmy had for the word "vacation."

"Come on," Qimmy yelled, distracting me from my explanation. She had gone to the block corner and was seated on the carpet we used for building. She took the bin of train tracks and the long wooden tunnels that had represented subways in her early play.

"Mommy and me ride the D train," she said with certainty. She assembled the tracks and tunnels.

"The D train takes you to your new house and the D train takes you back to day care and Queeny's house," I elaborated.

"The D train takes me back," she repeated.

I reached for some small people to use with the blocks. "You like to come back and see Queeny and Maria. Let's make where Queeny lives and where your school is and where your new house is."

Qimmy placed two female figures in a tunnel, then laid Queeny down on a block bed at one end of the long track. "Make school," she commanded. I made an enclosure near Queeny's roofless, wall-less house. Qimmy placed several people inside. She looked up at me.

"What about Opal and Qimmy's new house?" I inquired.

She thought for a minute. "That," she said, placing a flat board at the other end of the track.

"What's that part, Qimmy?"

"A floor. My bed is a floor at Mommy's new house. I sleep with a blanket."

That's right, I thought. Franklyn was having a hard time expediting the furniture allowance that welfare recipients could receive when entering housing. Queeny had provided extra blankets from her house to be both mattress and cover until the beds came.

I went and got a tissue from a box on the shelf. "Let's pretend that this is the blanket Queeny gave you to take to your new house." I laid the tissue over Qimmy's floor. "When you feel cold or you feel lonely for Queeny you can put your blanket on. Let's make Qimmy and Opal come home and try it."

We walked the dolls through the tunnel and they emerged on Qimmy's floor. Qimmy put the blanket over the Qimmy doll.

"Mommy, too," she instructed me, pointing to the tissues. I obediently got a blanket for Opal, who was then put to sleep beside Qimmy.

"Mommy cries," Qimmy said sadly. "Get more tissues." I brought the tissue box.

"Maybe you and Mommy need a lot of tissues in your new house for a while. Maybe you and Mommy feel lonely for Queeny. You're scared about being in a new place and Mommy cries."

Qimmy took many tissues from the box. She then picked up the two little figures, which were made of pegs with hollow centers, and began stuffing the tissues inside, filling the emptiness that each felt in their empty new home.

"Qimmy is making the dolls feel full," I said softly.

"They feel full tomorrow," Qimmy responded.

■ ■ ■

"Franklyn assured me that he will home-visit Opal this week and that the furniture will arrive imminently," I told Franny as we set up the room for the group. She patiently listened to my worries about patients, and I patiently listened to hers.

I had seen neither Opal nor Queeny since returning from my vacation, as the clinic schedule was very heavy in the fall. Queeny had reported by telephone that she was getting adequate care and Opal was making out all right.

"Don't worry," said Franny as she set cake-baking ingredients out on the table. "In five seconds the children will be here and all other concerns will seem nonexistent."

We had planned to bake a cake as our group activity, to be eaten in our next session, the last one together. Maimai, Angie, and Raquel had wanted strawberry and had managed to convince 'Mitri and Kendra to abandon their chocolate fantasies for the occasion. I refrained from talking them back into a chocolate fantasy for my own reasons.

We had gone out and gotten enough strawberry cake mix and strawberry frosting for a large flat pan. The door opened.

"Raquel's sick," they announced in unison.

Maimai took it from there. "Her mama said to tell you she wasn't comin.' " Maimai looked sad about this. 'Mitri looked stricken and Kendra looked angry. Angie had been put on a low dosage of Melleril, an anti-psychotic drug, to help her through the transition from group to day treatment. She was not accustomed to medication and looked drowsy and wan.

"Well, who's going to put the water in, then?" Kendra demanded. The water was Raquel's job.

"Raquel's gonna feel real bad if she don't get to do some," Maimai reflected. "Raquel my best friend."

Franny and I fell silent for a moment, realizing that we were witnessing the birth of empathy in Maimai. Angie sat in a chair next to Franny and put her head in Franny's lap.

"Well," 'Mitri said impatiently, "are we still going to make the cake or not? I don't have all day, you know." She was hovering around the eggs, desperate to be able to carry out the job she had been promised, but controlling herself.

"Maimai is worried that Raquel will feel bad if we do it without her, and 'Mitri is worried that we won't get a chance to do it at all. I'm worried that if we wait for Raquel we won't have time to eat our cake, because we only have one more session and cakes take a long time to bake."

"I know what to do," Kendra announced. "We can write Raquel a letter and tell her, 'We are sorry you couldn't come to put water into the cake, but we came anyway so we did it for you.' "

"Yeah, tell her she can eat some anyway," 'Mitri said magnanimously, "even though she didn't do nothin'."

Franny was taking this dictation down on a large piece of newsprint from the easel. "Now you guys can all sign your names," Franny suggested, "and we can give it to the bus driver and see if he will take it by Raquel's house for us." This satisfied everyone and they descended on the ingredients, Kendra carefully measuring her oil and Raquel's water, 'Mitri cracking the eggs so forcefully that the shells splintered into pieces, and Angie tasting her way through the mix of strawberry powder and batter.

'Mitri said something inaudible.

"What you said, 'Mitri?" Kendra inquired.

"None of your business," 'Mitri responded crossly.

"Kendra thought you were telling her something," I interjected. "Do you want to tell us something?"

"Just you," 'Mitri said to me. "It's a secret," she said fiercely in Kendra's direction.

I led 'Mitri to our supply closet, where private conferences sometimes took place. 'Mitri stood in the corner near the now deflated punching bag, her arms hugging her chest.

"I told my mama no," she whispered.

"You told your mama no about what?" I whispered back.

"I told her I ain't gonna be no lookout if she goes back to doin' you know what. I told her I'm staying home, that there ain't none of my business."

"What did Mommy say?" I looked into her once-confused and fragile face and listened to her feeling-filled voice speaking for herself.

"She said, 'All right then, I ain't gonna do that no more any old way.' She says she goin' to her program every day."

"How does that sound to you?"

"Sounds fine to me, but Miss O'Reilly better check and make sure, that's what I think."

"When Miss O'Reilly calls me, I'll tell her you'd like her to make sure."

'Mitri nodded her approval. She leaned back into the corner, looking up at me anxiously as if there was something else she wanted to say.

"Why did you spank Angie's butt the other day?" she asked finally.

"I spanked Angie because I was scared she would hurt herself. She couldn't listen to me right then and I had to stop her very fast, and that was the only way I could think of to stop her," I explained. "That must have scared you because you know I don't spank children."

"All right then. I knew it was something like that. I just was makin' sure, that's all," 'Mitri said, then hugged me quickly, relieved that there had been reason to my madness, and flung the door open. "I'm gonna put sprinkles on my piece of cake," she announced. "They gonna be chocolate."

■ ■ ■

"I got two letters," Ronnie said, bubbling. "The second one is an airplane ticket. He said I could come for the Jewish holidays or over Thanksgiving."

"Great."

"Grandma said she would take care of Sara," she whispered, as though Sara might hear her. Then she said, "Grandma said she didn't take good care of Sara when she was little. I don't believe her." She looked at me for affirmation but got neutrality, so she continued.

"Did you know Grandma escaped from the war when she was the same age as me?" she asked incredulously.

I nodded.

"I could never be that brave." She looked frozen for a moment, as if she might never leave my chair.

"Did Rena say she felt brave?"

Ronnie shook her head. "No, she said she was too young to go away alone. And she could never go back. Her parents were killed; she never saw them again." Her speech had become slow and deliberate.

"Rena was too young to go away alone. Teenagers like to practice going out and trying things on their own, but they're not ready for the real thing. They need to be able to come back home to their parents. Rena couldn't come back. The worst fear a child has about leaving her parents is that something bad will happen to them while she's away, and that's what happened to Rena when she was your age. Maybe she carried that fear to Sara when Sara was a teenager, and maybe Sara carried it to you."

Ronnie gave a nervous laugh. "Carrying fears. That's funny. Like the women in Haiti carrying baskets on their heads."

"Invisible baskets of fear, and it's hard to keep your balance when you're walking around with one," I commented.

"I'm going to make a painting of that," she promised, "in art class."

"I'd like to see that," I said.

She stopped talking for a few minutes and concentrated on making lines by running her finger through the bin full of corn-meal on the radiator next to her chair.

"I want to tell you something, but I'm afraid you're going to be mad," she said tentatively.

"Would you be afraid if I got mad?" I asked.

"Huh?" she said squinting, resisting my question. "I don't know. Just let me tell you." She tossed her red hair behind her in a grown-up way. "I'm ready to stop coming here," she said all in one breath. "I have journalism projects after school and vol-leyball." She stopped to look at my face. "Can I?"

"No," I said, "not yet."

She looked back at me incredulous. "Why?" she demanded, her eyes burning with anger.

"Because I think you need to keep talking about what hap-pens with you and your dad for a while, and because I think you should know more about what the invisible baskets of fear look like."

She gave me a fleeting sullen look, made voiceless by her anger.

And, I thought, you need a lot more practice being angry.

"It's not fair," she said finally in a controlled voice, "that you get to decide."

"I know," I agreed. "And now it's you who's angry."

She struggled to keep her tears from spilling over. "Well, when do you think I can stop?" she asked in a voice detached from feeling.

"I don't think it's so far off. I think we could work once a week instead of twice for a while and see how that goes. You can see if you feel like you have enough time to talk about what comes up here and also see your friends and do your school activities. After Christmastime we'll talk about it again and de-cided together."

Ronnie looked very relieved. Relieved that there was an end in sight, relieved that I wouldn't let her disappear.

"I think Grandma thinks I'm going to get depressed when I get older like Sara did," Ronnie blurted out. "Am I?"

"What makes you think Rena thinks you'll get depressed like Sara?"

"She told me I should keep coming here for a long time and . . . I still get scared sometimes." She groped for words.

"Being scared doesn't make a person depressed. Everyone feels scared sometimes." I took a deep breath, suddenly feeling chilled by Ronnie's courage. "Remember you said that Rena was brave coming to America?"

Ronnie nodded.

"I think you could feel brave about letting the shadow lady and the troll and the igloo and all those scary images come out so they didn't have to stay hidden inside of you. That's what makes people depressed, when their feelings stay hidden from themselves. Rena knows that by coming here you've gotten really good at uncovering your feelings for yourself, and I think she's very proud of you for that."

Ronnie beamed. "You too?" she asked shyly.

"Me too," I said, smiling.

"Then I'll see you next week," she said with pride, and took her brave self home.

■   ■   ■

The last day of group was an October day that one New York City weatherman called "one of the ten best days of the year." The sky was Crayola blue, with a brilliant sun that touched the chilly air but didn't smother it. Fan-shaped leaves had turned yellow but still clung to their branches, making mustard-colored umbrellas for people walking by in the street.

I was heading toward the subway with seven colors of cake-decorating icing in my bag, one for each child and one each for Franny and me. The crispness of the day and the intensity of the occasion combined to create an inner dizziness, as though I were walking on air, but with pockets full of paperweights slowing my pace.

The subway platform was crammed with commuters eager to stand in the path of the cool breeze blowing in from the street grates. Express trains whizzed by and local ones stopped, taking large portions of the crowd with them, leaving only the shadow people behind to sit on the benches or board the trains when the aisles were clear enough for begging. When the train doors closed me in, I insulated myself from their neediness, shutting myself off for privacy, and let a dreamlike state transport me to the group good-bye.

The bus came late, delivering the kids in a strangely quiet and compliant state, each wearing dresses, as they had instructed Franny and me to do as well. Raquel was there, although her eyes shone with a slight fever that the Tylenol she was taking could not suppress. Angie looked slightly more wakeful than last time and sat down on a chair next to me, holding on to my skirt with one hand and sucking her thumb.

'Mitri, Kendra, Raquel, Maimai, and Angie gathered around the cake, which Franny and I had decorated with all of our names. They were awed that the symbols of their identities could be inscribed and then consumed by them, the rightful owners. There were also small dishes of every flavor of sprinkles, M&Ms, and Red Hots for each to use in decorating her piece of cake. The girls were deeply absorbed in the creation of their special designs, eating handfuls of decorations as they worked.

Raquel broke the silence with one question that no one had asked yet. "You all have new kids when we don't come back no more?" she inquired, her decorated piece of cake in hand.

I answered her honestly in spite of the pull to deny that other children would have access to what they considered their own. "We have to wait until the kindergarten teachers decide if there are any new children who need our group," I explained. They considered this awhile as they passed around cups of juice.

"They'll even get our own storybooks?" Maimai asked indignantly. There was one about a baby learning to use the potty that she especially liked.

"Maybe some kids will use the same stories you liked, and maybe some kids will like other stories," Franny answered.

"They won't know *nothin'* about this group," 'Mitri said possessively.

"Maybe we should write them a story so they'll know how to use the group," I thought out loud.

'Mitri sprang from her seat and positioned herself at the

easel. "You'll talk and I'll write it down," she said, imitating
Franny, who usually did the writing.

"No," whined Angie. "She don't know how to spell it."

"I do too," 'Mitri countered furiously.

"I got an idea," Franny intervened. "How about if the kids
tell me what to write, and I write the story down and 'Mitri paints
a picture about it."

"Yeah," they agreed, " 'Mitri draws good." The compliment
satisfied 'Mitri, who went to work.

"Wait!" screamed Maimai. "You don't know what it's gonna
be about yet."

"Let's start, 'Once upon a time we had a group,' " suggested
Kendra.

"Only five people are allowed 'cause it would be too
crowded," Angie inserted.

"Five people can come even if they pee on theirselves,"
Maimai contributed.

"But you can't bite," Angie added solemnly.

"You could have a bottle as long as you act your age eventually," 'Mitri said in a wise tone. Franny and I stifled laughter as
Franny wrote down each word faithfully.

"You can have friends," said Raquel simply.

"You can play grown-up," Kendra said, "like being a nun or
a ballet dancer or that you have a store with a lot of candy."

"Other peoples might cry and get on your nerves, but it's not
like they dyin' or nothin'," Maimai pointed out, taking a huge
bite of cake.

"If they do get on your nerves, you can ask for some privacy,"
'Mitri put in.

"Or bring them some potato chips so they can be your
friend," Angie dictated as she licked icing.

"Or if someone hurted you, you can tell," Kendra contributed, looking at me for affirmation.

"Okay," screamed 'Mitri. "That's enough. I can't paint no
more on one paper!"

We all shifted our attention to 'Mitri's easel, which held five
little girls' faces surrounded by deep blues and purples, threaded
with a few strings of orange, like sunset after a storm.

"Ohhhhh," sang Maimai and Raquel with true admiration. 'Mitri smiled brilliantly.

■ ■ ■

The phone was ringing as I turned the key in the lock. I heard my machine begin to answer; then I interrupted it.

"Hi," Betsy's voice said.

"How do you always know the exact minute I'll be coming home?" I asked.

"ESP," she answered, "but I'm not calling for myself. I've got Opal over here. She'd like to come over and see you in your office and ask you about something."

I was speechless. Betsy's voice communicated her amusement. "I explained to her that you had offices at the clinic and a private office, and that the clinic office might be better in the long run, but since she'd like a session right away I thought maybe I could send her over now."

"Sure," I finally managed to say. "Is she okay?"

She responded patiently, "She's right here with me."

"Fine," I said, collecting myself. "Tell her she should be here in fifteen minutes." I hung up, realizing that Opal had never asked me for anything except, of course, her initial request for day care for Qimmy. I felt anxious as I sat awaiting her arrival.

The bell finally rang, and I was surprised when the opened door revealed a bouncing Qimmy as well as an apprehensive Opal.

"Come in," I said brightly, leading them to the treatment room. Qimmy skipped ahead of me and Opal lingered behind. I turned to wait for her and she motioned me closer.

"Qimmy wanted to come with me, but I need to talk to you alone," she said in a hushed tone. I nodded and intercepted Qimmy before she got too attached to the room, whisking her into the hallway with a Fisher-Price house and a bag of blocks.

"You can play here and watch Mommy and me through the glass door," I told her. She sat cross-legged, becoming absorbed in the toys.

Opal arranged her African skirt over the edges of the butterfly chair. She had a matching scarf on her head that was tied on the side and hung down over her shoulder. Her hands were

resting on the sides of the chair and her eyes were hiding under
heavy lids.

"How have things been going for you?" I began.

"All right," she answered briefly.

"How about Queeny?" I tried again.

"She tired, sleepin' a lot, but she all right."

I decided to wait and let her tell me when she got ready.
We sat.

"What I'm worried about is Qimmy," she said finally.
"Qimmy is goin' through something that makes her curious
about everything."

"She wants to know why everything in the world is the way it
is," I paraphrased.

Opal nodded. "Why this and why that," she elaborated.

"She has figured out that things happen for a reason. It'll
help her when she goes to kindergarten to be able to ask questions and understand cause and effect," I explained in an animated way. The development of Qimmy's "why's" were exciting
to me.

Opal nodded again, this time sadly.

"But there's something sad about that for you, I gather," I
said, trying to follow her mood.

"She want to know why she don't have no daddy," Opal said
in a hollow voice.

"Hmmm," I answered. I had no idea what the story of
Qimmy's father was. "What did you say?"

"I told her to go look at TV and we would talk about that
another time."

I smiled at Opal's use of age-old delaying tactics. "That's a
hard one to answer. It's probably a complicated story," I guessed.

"Too complicated," Opal confirmed, "but Qimmy don't forget nothin' lately. She might ask again tomorrow." She fingered
the magnetic sculpture tentatively.

"You're worried about what to say," I reflected.

Opal nodded again miserably. "Sometimes I remember
things folks told me when I was a girl. About why I didn't have no
mother. It didn't make no sense most of the time. Then they say
the truth right out to one another like I wasn't even there. Only

Queeny told me the truth and not until I was grown." Her eyes filled with tears.

"Only Queeny told the truth and she won't be able to tell it for many more years," I said, giving Opal's sadness a voice.

Opal began crying noisless tears, nodding.

"So maybe you feel like you need to find your own version of the truth," I continued, "so you'll have something to tell Qimmy." She wiped her face with a tissue from the box next to her. We sat in silence.

"So I was thinking maybe I could come and see you for a while," she said tentatively, "to talk about what we gonna say to Qimmy when she ask 'why this' and 'why that.' "

I smiled at her use of "we." "Good idea," I agreed, beaming. "I've got to look at my calendar and then call you so we can schedule a time."

"Okay."

"Let's go see what Qimmy is doing," I proposed. We peered around the corner and saw Qimmy playing on the other side of the glass door. There was a tiny enclosure of blocks behind the Fisher-Price house with a window big enough for two little people to peek from. Qimmy was carefully covering the tiny dwelling with a flat block just the right size for a roof. Then, seeing the finished product, she clapped her hands in self-congratulation. When she saw us watching her through the glass, she pointed with pride at the new home she had created.

EPILOGUE

This garden really *is* a jungle garden. The leaves are huge enough to shut out the sky if I look up beyond the banana palms and the akee trees that provide refuge from the noonday sun. I have never known sun like this. The winter renders it gentle but persistent, and in spite of my number-30 sunscreen, my skin is coated with a golden-marshmallow tan that will serve as evidence that I actually went on a vacation to have fun. What fantasies will my patients have about this?

My hair has been braided in cornrows by women who live down the road and make their living this way. It hurt each time the hair was pulled into place. I thought of all the little girls I have known who were "tender-headed." "It hurts to be beautiful," my unsympathetic braider advised me.

The visa papers that they gave me at the airport say "Runaway Bay, Jamaica—6 nights, 7 days." In Biblical times, a week seemed sufficient for creating a new world. I wondered if it would be long enough for me to grow comfortable in a domain that feels more dangerous than New York City's subways—a "for singles" domain. Last night I wore a black flowered outfit with colored glass buttons and sat at a piano bar drinking Kahlúa and cream, singing until one in the morning. I did not have dreams about children.

This morning I snorkeled over a coral reef and visited schools of round, striped yellow fish and frilly, black velvet ones. They all seemed to regard me as a larger version of themselves and welcomed me into their underwater home. In contrast, the colorful but foreboding coral caves seemed to warn: "I'd turn back if I were you."

I thought about it. For years, caves of fear prevented me from creating my own version of home and family, simultaneously compelling me to hold the hands of others who needed help themselves. Today I hovered over the coral caves for a while, refusing to be intimidated. A fish came out and blew bubbles at me.